THE
JOY
of the
Disinherited

**ESSAYS ON TRAUMA, OPPRESSION,
AND BLACK MENTAL HEALTH**

KEVIN DEDNER

Murphy, Timoteo, *Disinherited Journeys*, 2021,
pigment paint, watercolor, acrylic paint on master paper

Contents

Acknowledgments

This work would not be possible without the support of my family. I am grateful for the sacrifices of Olivia, Davis, Ella, Anna, my mother, brother, and sister. They know that I've missed important events and been at others with my mind somewhere else. Still, they have given me the grace and space to write this book. I am also grateful for my colleagues at Hurdle and our ecosystem of investors and supporters. Our shared vision for knocking down invisible barriers to mental health care has, in part, empowered my courage to share my story.

A few years back, I was interviewed by journalist Nicole Clark, a senior writer for StartUp Health at the time. I can't explain why, but I instantly knew we'd be connected indefinitely. Over the years, Nicole conducted follow-up interviews, tracking the evolution of my digital health start-up, Hurdle. In 2020, she called to tell me she was going out on her own as a freelancer, and I invited her to do some work for Hurdle. I told her about this debt that I owed the universe and my desire to share the deeper story—my story— behind my efforts in the mental health space. She agreed to join me, and we have been laboring together since that conversation. Her skill and professionalism are unmatched, and this work would not be possible without her. With Nicole, I have been able to build an incredibly talented team for this book. Dantavious Hicks served as the lead researcher, chiefly responsible for the reference section. Together, we combed through each essay looking for the clinical significance of some of my life experiences. His mentor, Dr. Norma Day-Vines, did a clinical review. Dr. Day-Vines is also intimately involved in the work of Hurdle. Alana Galbert, a summer intern at Hurdle and entering freshman at James Madison University, also supported the research work. I am also thankful for the tutelage of Carolyn Henderson Allen, Janis Kearney, Jajuan Johnson, Masie Cochran, and Patrice Gaines. Patrice introduced me to Mae Israel, who served as my developmental editor. Mae pushed me on the meaning of my words, and you are reading a better manuscript because of her. Syd Hayman copy edited the manuscript.

In the early days, I set out to find a publisher for this work. After months of searching and conversations, I came to terms with the limitations of the publishing industry—the traditional timelines from concept to publication, the barriers to entry as a first-time author—and I decided to self-publish. I formed a company to do so, My Own Holdings, named in honor of my ancestor MackinTosh Dedner. On Ancestry.com, I found a copy of his 1917-18 World War I registration card. On that card, he listed his occupation as a farmer. The card also has a space for his employer. That line simply reads, "My Own." Papa Mack was farming land that had been passed on to him by his father, James Dedner. James Dedner was born into slavery and later purchased 156 acres in Lockesburg, Arkansas, on January 23, 1899, through the federal Homestead Act.

My hope is that this book will serve as a tribute to all my ancestors and a light for future generations.

Rev. Dr. Otis Moss III

At 12 years of age, I sat with my family on the second pew of the Olivet Institutional Baptist Church in Cleveland, Ohio. Rev. Andrew Jackson Young Jr., a renowned civil rights leader, minister, and former ambassador to the United Nations, offered the morning message to celebrate our church's anniversary. I cannot recall the message. I was in a pre-teen fog of hopeful prayer, occasionally dozing off. I wanted the service to end quickly so I could eat, connect with friends, and watch the Cleveland Browns give the city a cardiac arrest: either by barely winning a game in the fourth quarter or brilliantly losing in the last two minutes.

Despite my youthful ambivalence, that Sunday took on special significance. Following the service, I waited patiently in my father's office for Rev. Young and my father, Otis Moss Jr., who was the pastor of Olivet, to return from the reception following the worship service. After what seemed to be an eternity, Rev. Young and my father entered the office after greeting parishioners. I gathered my coat, a typical passive-aggressive pre-teen signal to say, "Let's go Pop!" Rev. Young paused, looked in my direction, and said, "Little Otis, have you read Howard Thurman?" I thought to myself, "I'm twelve, why would I read Howard Thurman?" I heard the name often mentioned by my parents. I knew he was a minister, a philosopher of sorts.

Unless their last name was King, or their first name was Stephen, Lee or Stan, they did not occupy significant real estate on my bookshelf. I answered Rev. Young with a quiet, "No, sir." He placed his hand on my shoulder and spoke words that changed my personal library, and subsequently, my life. "Otis, he is one of our greatest thinkers. I want you to go into your father's study and get a copy of *Jesus and the Disinherited*. I want you to read the book. It is very short; when you finish, call me and we will talk about it." I nodded and whispered, "Yes, sir." That evening, I asked my father for the book and placed it at my bedside. It sat there for weeks. Eventually, I opened the book and each night I read a few passages. I would love to share with you a child prodigy story, one in which I read the entire book and became a pre-teen Thurman disciple, but my reception and application of Thurman's teachings happened over time. However, those nights spent reading passages of *Jesus and the Disinherited* as a seventh and eighth grader were the moment his luminous ideas became enshrined in my psyche.

Later, as a college student, I devoured Thurman's work. I spent many evenings with my father discussing this prophet and mystic who interrogated evangelical doctrine and simultaneously offered a new vision of spirituality for the American democratic project. This spiritual giant was arguably one the greatest, if not, the most influential spiritual thinker in America. Yet, he is unfortunately not widely known among the general public. His influence upon Dr. Martin Luther King Jr.'s theology, Dr. Vincent Harding's approach to history, Alice Walker's literary vision, Derek Bell's critical race legal theory, and Harry Belafonte's artistry cannot be understated.

Thurman deserves to be placed in the sacred pantheon of our greatest spiritual teachers. It will be a tragedy if a new generation does not wrestle with the earth-shaking power of his spiritual teaching. Thurman was shaped by the Black sacred tradition cultivated by his mother and grandmother. He had a spiritual lens that western religiosity is often blind to witness. Two profound and thoughtful Black women were his first teachers, giving him an unconscious, yet prominent womanist filter to examine America's spiritual strivings. He drew from the well of Black spirituality that also reshaped the harsh, and at times, tragic doctrine of white evangelicalism. His southern, rural upbringing allowed him to develop an organic mysticism that witnessed God's power and beauty manifesting through nature. These roots pushed him to develop a theological approach that was unafraid of different traditions or agnostic frames of living. He was always in search of common ground among all human beings that allowed people to flourish and live out one's purpose while speaking truth.

The book you hold is a publication I wish had been available to my middle school teachers. Works such as this would have revolutionized my early education in Social Studies, American History, and Introduction to World Religions classes, and powerfully informed my doctorate and ministerial studies. In *The Joy of the Disinherited*, Kevin Dedner dares to take the work of this giant, and pass on the prophet's legacy to a new generation. In his autobiography, Thurman eloquently presents the complexity of his own spiritual and personal identity formation. He unpacks how to "manage the carking fear of the white man's power and not be defeated by our own rage and hatred." Dedner's noble endeavor to resurrect Thurman's teachings within a poetic and articulate discourse on Black self-esteem and mental health—recurring themes in Thurman's books—will be a blessing for years to come. I know this book will not only challenge you, but put you on the path to find your own growing edge, and centering moment within the hectic and noisy world of today. It will ignite a journey to rediscover a joy that has long been your rightful inheritance, a joy that no one can take from you.

—Rev. Dr. Otis Moss III, Senior Pastor of Trinity United Church of Christ in Chicago, Illinois

The Practice of Remembering

"This is my historical life—my singular, special example
that is personal, but that also represents the race."

—HENRY BIBB, 1849

I start my mornings slow and quiet. Some days, I must fight for the quiet, fight to slow my thoughts. When my to-do list runs pages-long, a mental tug-of-war ensues between my need for stillness and the demands of work. Stillness always wins, protected by some subconscious biological drive toward survival. My well-being depends on these slow, quiet, early moments of the day. Morning is a sacred and hallowed time where I can come as I am. It is the space where I connect with myself. I have no agenda. Only to make allowance and time to commune with my Creator. Sometimes I reach out to a friend or mentor if I need to hear another voice. The list is short, but there are people I know I can call on: Frank Scott Jr., Melvin Maxwell, and my older brother, Billy. I used to call my dear friend and mentor Leroy Brownlee before he passed away. In these phone calls, we discuss existential matters—scripture, theology, philosophy. We allow ourselves to be vulnerable. We share questions and doubts about our life purpose and sentiments on how well or not we are existing in it.

A confession: I have long questioned my purpose. I have spent many nights that turned into early mornings worrying about whether I would discover my purpose soon enough to do anything about it. I have long willed myself to be both the protagonist and hero of my own story. One day, I imagined, I would wake to find myself firmly planted at the center of my life's purpose, so long as I kept on the straight and narrow. I can hear my preacher's words: "We all have a purpose in God, Kevin." I believe that. For myself, for others. But over time, I have come to believe that our life's purpose mirrors the inherent rhythms of life. It evolves. Purpose is not a destination, but a journey.

One day, I woke up in the basement of my home, lost and uncentered. This morning, as I write this, it is Father's Day 2021. I am found, centered in a purpose greater than the sum of all my imaginings: revolutionizing America's mental health system as we know it. The only sounds are my breath and a bird's song. I did not arrive at this point without hurt and pain. Mine has been an eventful life. So has yours. None of us get to move through life without experiencing some pain and hurt, some trauma. Sadly, most of us are not adequately equipped to understand our trauma, let alone prepared to move through it into the light. In the following essays, I share how I made the journey from dark to light, from discouragement to intention.

At first, I set out to write a book about the health of Black men. I desperately wanted to raise awareness about how Black men live sicker and shorter lives than anyone. I'd seen it firsthand in the premature death of my father, then father figures. In the early deaths of Black male mentors, friends, family members. I mourned them. I grieved our reality. At times, I did so publicly. I published essays that tied my work in public health and mental health care to my own personal experience as a Black man. But writing a book took rhythm. For years, all I had to offer was a syncopated scat lamenting the unfair ask of Black men to cope against all odds. I look back now and understand I needed to live a few more chapters into the future to find that rhythm. America needed its racial past raked across the coals in a year like 2020. Over time, the vision and idea of the book have evolved into what it is today—a memoir of essays. Each essay could stand alone. In this way, some aspects of my life's story are repeated in each essay for the sake of context. The scope of my storytelling is intentionally narrow. Rather than an autobiography that chronicles my life from cradle to present day, focus is given to anecdotes that show how oppression skewed my family's identity development and my own. The nonlinear and inquisitive essay form allows for an honest exploration into how I deconstructed toxic misbeliefs to grow into the person I am today. When you read these essays, you join this exploration. You are tracing my steps. Together, we observe how I forgave my past self and the broken world that raised me so that I might lay claim to the vision of who I am meant to be.

—

Mornings have a way of reminding us that life, above all else, goes on. Forever moving forward, not backward. Nonetheless, I have wished for a do-over more times than I can recall. I have wanted a clean slate. For my mistakes and ignorances to be washed away, for lost loved ones to return. To start again, to try again. In the mornings, I return to this age-old promise: This too shall pass. I embrace the heartaches while they linger, knowing they will fade and leave in their place the lessons that have shaped me.

Lessons are what advance us in life and writing this book has offered both joyful and painful ones. I dug deep to understand my trauma, to come to terms with how I have treated people and how they have treated me. As a child, I believed that Black people were oddly placed in the world. I learned this belief through the images and articles in the *Ebony* and *Jet* magazines my mother would leave on the coffee table, and in the encyclopedias my grandmother would stack against the walls in my home. I learned this through the unspoken racial codes of the South that my elders subtly modeled. Juxtaposed to this understanding of my odd place in the world was a pervasive belief that God loves Black people and has not forsaken us. My ancestors passed down this belief, and elders nurtured it, instilling it in me. These two opposing beliefs would eventually require an examination of my own mind. It would require what Rev. Howard Thurman refers to as a "surgical examination of the psyche." A parsing of misbelief from truth with the precision of a surgeon.

When I first came across the work of Thurman—a philosopher, civil rights leader, and one of the most influential theologians of the twentieth century—my life changed. I was inspired to learn that Martin Luther King Jr. studied and traveled with his book *Jesus and the Disinherited*. It was the capstone of years of struggle and study for me. My public health career provided me with an intellectual understanding of health and health disparities. Firsthand encounters with oppression and discrimination marked my life. Personal mental health challenges led me to therapy and then to study mental health. But it wasn't until I read *Jesus and the Disinherited* that I obtained the necessary framework to intellectually and spiritually understand the impact of oppression on the minds and bodies of the oppressed.

Thurman's book frames Jesus's teachings as meant especially for the "disinherited." It extends far beyond typical theological pontifications, positioning Jesus as a historic revolutionary in the context of an oppressive Roman empire. In this regard, the disinherited represent a people who the power structure or ruling class have relegated to an inferior—an odd—position in society. In the book, Thurman argues there are three ways the disinherited deal with oppression. They either:

1. take on a general plan for nonresistance, one of imitation

2. reduce contact with the oppressor to a minimum

3. employ "the other major alternative": resistance

In *The Joy of the Disinherited*, I use this resistance framework to declare that Black people are the "disinherited" of America due to our inequitable relationship with the country. In some places, I extend the definition of the disinherited to Black *and Brown* people. In these places, my intent is not to umbrella the unique experiences of various minorities in America, but to simply extend a sympathetic notion of understanding to those who, like me, have been oppressed at one time or another because of the color of their skin. I pull heavily from Thurman's philosophies and quote him often. Through an asynchronous storytelling style, I offer you my story and the story of my family as vulnerable examples of the disinherited's unresolved generational trauma. Regardless of the position the disinherited takes (resistance or nonresistance), there are negative consequences to psychological health. In each essay, I share with you the ways my family and I demonstrated Thurman's forms of resistance and nonresistance and our personal consequences.

Mary-Frances Winters wrote in her 2020 book *Black Fatigue*, "The health disparities that exist among Black people are well researched. But they are not well known." To narrow this knowledge gap, I've included an unconventional reference section of empirical research and studies from the 1970s through today that document links between racism and health outcomes. This reference section serves as a supportive brace to my personal narrative, offering some of the same research that I uncovered years ago during my search to understand the unique ways depression and anxiety show up in Black men and the broader disinherited community.

Finally, I share how I have been conditioned as a son of the South and my self-examination of my psyche. This self-examination is required for the disinherited to unearth our humane inheritance. In this way, I wrote this book first for myself, and then for you. The process of writing supported my continued healing from living as a Black man in America. I am afraid that this healing will be necessary for as long as I live. For every time a sore is close to healing, there is another police shooting of a Black person, a racial injustice that knocks the scab off, and the healing process starts all over again. However, with the close of each essay in this book, I came to know myself and the iterative healing process better.

I looked to literary ancestors and historic agitators I admire for inspiration—James Baldwin, Rev. Howard Thurman, Martin Luther King Jr., Malcolm X, and Toni Morrison—as well as modern-day thought leaders and poets Ibram X. Kendi, Hanif

Abdurraqib, and Elizabeth Alexander. I identified my own injurious thought patterns and, where relevant, their oppressive, racist origins. I challenged—and in many cases, destroyed—those ill-founded thoughts and rebuilt my own intellectually investigated beliefs. I advanced into the light by making space to remember and reflect on my dark moments. Where necessary, I dispossessed parts of my selfhood that had developed under the weight of oppression. I remembered where I came from and rediscovered myself. I connected to something bigger by being still enough to tell my story. I have written it with the hope that I can offer a story that hasn't been told—yet is worthy of being heard.

Sacrificial Love

"You gotta call on that something that your daddy used to tell you about. That power that can make a way out of no way."

—MARTIN LUTHER KING JR.,
"Why Jesus Called a Man a Fool (Sermon)," 1967

I rarely talk about my father's death. His death was tragic, the kind you learn to keep quiet. First, there was a long addiction, then an abrupt passage from here to the by-and-by. By the time I was a teenager, I learned the art of silence when friends complained about their dads. Though, I wanted to grab their shoulders and whisper in their ear, "Love the ones you got while you got 'em."

That I am tied to my father's story—his unresolved trauma, his addictions, his death—is never more apparent to me than when I am dealing with my own children. They are growing up fast in a world that will surely misunderstand them, be it for the color of their skin, the curl in their hair, or the white of their eyes. This is why I make an exception for Anna, Ella, and Davis. I tell them the story of my daddy's death. I resurrect his story in hopes that together we can bind ourselves to a beautiful, albeit tragic, flowering of love and life after death.

I tell them how Daddy died unexpectedly at Christmastime.
I was ten years old.
The year was 1986.
I lived in Little Rock, Arkansas.
There was snow on the ground.

I remember the snow because it, too, was unlooked for. Little Rock rarely sees temperatures dip below freezing. When the cold comes, it seldom sticks around long enough to keep a snowscape from turning to mud. What I'm saying is that even if I had not buried my father under a skift of Southern snow, I still would have remembered the white ground in Arkansas that year. Kids remember when the world looks like a Kodak moment. And they remember when their world fades to black.

—

Late in the evening on Christmas Eve, I peeked around the corner of the brick wall separating my bedroom from the kitchen. I was eavesdropping. My mother was giving my father a good shakedown over the phone—"giving him a piece of my mind," as she'd say—reminding him of the money he'd promised us, the money for gifts for me, my brother, Billy, and my sister, Cynthia. It was a peace offering we'd come to expect each December from Daddy. It was the one time of year when the world, or at least Radio Shack, was our oyster.

By 1986, I'd grown used to living without a father. I had come to believe, like Daddy did, that money could pull us out of the sadness of his absence. It was just all too heavy to bear otherwise. Which is why whenever the money went dry, the fire between him and my mother burned hot. That year on Christmas

Eve, their disagreement was especially fevered. They couldn't seem to agree if Christmas was tomorrow or two days away. Eventually, I grew tired of snooping and dozed off.

Christmas came and went. Two days later, another disquieting phone call. This time it was Daddy's brother Jerry calling to say that Daddy was in the hospital drifting in and out of consciousness. My father had suffered a cocaine-induced brain aneurysm. Later, I learned that when he and my mother exchanged words over the phone on Christmas Eve, Daddy's mind was mush. He had no idea what day it was, but he was certain he still had time to make good on his promise to us.[1] After a short conversation, my mother pressed the telephone receiver into its wall mount. Then, she quickly dressed Billy, Cynthia, and me in every piece of warm clothing she could find. She ushered us into the car. As the ignition whined against the cold, the radio blared. "We Are the World" spilled out through the speakers. We sped north on Twelfth Street toward Little Rock's University Hospital while Lionel, Michael, Diana, and Stevie assured me that love was all I needed. Our muses whisper prophecies to us when the din of life is loudest. That night, I imagined these artists assembling like a great cloud of witnesses above me. From their vantage point in the heavens, I imagined them looking on, following the beams of light from our car under the black sky.

I spent the week between Christmas and New Year's Day in and out of the hospital at my father's bedside. I hummed the lyrics to "We Are the World" to the rhythm of the beeps and gasps from Daddy's life support system. *We are the children. We are the ones who make a brighter day, so let's start giving.* Before the year's end, he would be gone.

—

If all you know of me is my father's death, then all you know is what America has told you to believe about people who look like me. That I am one of millions—millions of Black men who lost their father too soon to too many drugs in an American city with too much crime.

Here, then, is where I beg you to perform mental gymnastics. If I tell you the story of my father's inelegant death, will you also see his proud, acceptable demands for individuality? Beyond my mother's sacrifices to create a new rhythm of life for her nerve-snapped children, will you also see how she rose from those ashes with the brilliance of a phoenix? Will you see the sacrifices of generations of men and women before her who stood with their backs against the wall, touched yet unpinned by the surging currents of Black life in the antebellum and postbellum South? Will you hear the story of my father's death without sacrificing my individuality on the altar of convenient stereotypes? Will you see that I am also one *in* a million?

We have long been told to believe in the mirage of biological racial differences and racial ancestry. It is "one of those widely held racist beliefs that few people realize they hold," writes scholar and author Ibram X. Kendi in *How to Be an Antiracist*[2]. Race, this ancient construct of power, this ideological handmaiden of slavery, has for millennia been fed by religion and science alike. Understandably, then, my asking you to parse Black eccentricity from Black sameness is no small task. I know this firsthand.

When the Black Lives Matter call first echoed in the streets of American cities in 2013, I realized with great pain in my heart that I, too, had made that gratuitous connection between biology and behavior. Quietly, though routinely, I would render demarcations of "me" and "them" among my Black brethren. I told myself that my mannered disposition was unblemished by the narrative told about Black men on the five o'clock news—I was not them; they were not me. But beneath my polished temperament were turbulent waters. Kendi says denial is the heartbeat of racism, and it beats in each of us, "beating across ideologies, races, and nations." For years, I denied the humanity of men who looked like me. For years, I denied my own father this humanity, even in his death. For years, the heartbeat of racism rattled against the walls of my own skin.[3]

—

There was a time when my mother and father celebrated Christmas under one roof. For ten years, they were hitched to each other's sides, their three children in tow.

Ophelia and Billy met as teenagers in Tucker, Arkansas. Tucker was and still is an unincorporated farm community in Jefferson County. Located forty minutes south of Little Rock, the northern tip of Jefferson County is the cradle of my maternal lineage. Specifically, Tucker and the town of Sherrill, and the nearly five-mile stretch of country along Arkansas Highway 15 that connects them. My mother's ancestors worked this farmland as sharecroppers, then as paid help. Time moves slower in these pockets of America. Little has changed here since John Woodfin Tucker established the Tucker Plantation in 1871. These are the things that have changed: the clothes people wear, the general store (it is in ruins), and the machinery used to pick cotton—doffers and conveyors instead of human hands.

Sherrill is the birthplace of my mother. For the first years of my mother's life, she and her parents, Ella Mae and George Gibson, lived in a home not theirs, a home situated on the Albright's land. The Albright's were one of ten well-to-do white families in Sherrill. They owned a large amount of land and were employers to families like mine, families of the disinherited. Ella Mae worked as a maid to Ada Albright, while my grandfather, George, worked as a farmhand for William Albright. By the time my mother was eleven, George had saved enough money to purchase a plot of land seven miles up the road in Tucker. There, he built a modest house. It would become a departure point for my family's eventual exodus from the country to the city.

My father came from a different Arkansas farming community. Two hundred miles southwest of Tucker, six miles from the Louisiana border, is Bradley, my father's hometown. In the late '60s, by the time he was old enough to drive, he would travel several hours from Bradley to Tucker once a year to visit his Uncle Glenn. Daddy would stay in Tucker for weeks at a time. It was his sanctuary, a repass from the hard life and abuse he experienced in his own home.

During one of those visits, he met my mother. Uncle Glenn lived next door to my mother's family. At first, my mother and father would trade looks out of the windows of their respective homes. Later, they'd meet under a nearby plum tree. Together, they'd imagine escaping the cotton fields that had for generations been a means to some bleary end for their families.

It is tempting to look back at history and read it with a certain inevitability. It is tempting to believe that my parents were destined for novelty. By the time they exchanged dreams of the future under that plum tree, the twentieth century civil rights movement had peaked and waned. Martin and Malcolm were in the ground by then, but their words lingered, inviting Black youth like my parents to a future of their own design. My mother and father's families had for generations planted seed, twisted cotton from burrs, and worked the gin. Ophelia and Billy would uproot. They would be the generation to leave the old plantation lands of Tucker and Bradley. They decided the city of Little Rock was where they could make a new life for themselves. Barely out of their teens, Ophelia and Billy were expectant parents. The city was a stone's throw away from their respective farm towns, but to them, Little Rock was the new world.

They married a few months before my older brother, Billy, was born in 1973. "Marrying is what you did in those situations," my mother says. "Having a baby out of wedlock was never an option." A year later, my mother completed an internship at the University of Arkansas at Little Rock and was offered a job as a receptionist. "The only Black person on the entire floor, and they sat me behind a glass wall for everyone to see." In 1976, I was born. By the time she was pregnant with Cynthia in 1980, she and her white coworkers had developed an amicable relationship. They threw her "the biggest baby shower ever seen." When Cynthia was born, my mother's coworkers asked her to bring Cynthia for a visit. "I don't think they'd ever seen a Black baby," my mother recalls. "They passed her around and started undressing her before I politely took her back in my arms." That same year, my parents moved to a house on Fair Park Boulevard, walking distance from the college campus.

No single memory I have points to a time when things changed for my father, and then for our family. I do know that the home on Fair Park holds my only memories of the five of us living together. At Christmastime, we'd place a pre-lit plastic tree from K-Mart in the corner of the living room. On Christmas Day, we'd gather around it, exchange red and green stockings stuffed with Primrose's hard candy from the Dollar General, and tear into our gifts—the latest remote-controlled car, new clothes, or an Atari console. They were always the kind of gifts that could change your entire image in school.

In 1984, we spent our first Christmas without Daddy. By this point, he was renting a shotgun house in Midtown, less than a mile from the historic Little Rock Central High School, on a street called Appianway.[4] He had an addition put on the home, a glorified closet where he'd keep his product. A bold move, but that was Daddy. On nights when my mother attended school at the University of Arkansas at Little Rock, we'd stay with my father. Daddy's record player would spin vinyl as his clients floated in and out. This was before the crack epidemic made hand-to-hand transactions on corners in blighted neighborhoods ubiquitous. Before the panache of the deal succumbed to the desperation of the client. Daddy's cocaine clients, for all intents and purposes, were reputable. They were people of all persuasions and socioeconomic means who liked to sit on his couch, talk music, and argue about President Reagan's politics. We knew the business could be brutal. My father often kept a revolver on the coffee table, and we learned early not to ask questions—not of my father, not of his clients, and not of his business partners who we would meet on my father's "runs."

In her charitable form, my mother will tell you that she and my father divorced because they were "moving in different directions," that they "wanted different things out of life," and that "sometimes adults just grow apart." On these days, she will tell you their divorce was "amicable." When she is feeling less generous and gets to twirling the hair at the nape of her neck, my mother will eke out a script that is different but equally true: "That straitlaced small-town farm boy that I fell in love with got a taste of the city," and "Your Daddy just couldn't get enough of it." It was her way of politely excusing my father for his addictions. It was the city's fault that he couldn't stay rooted in one place, not his. As a child, I wondered if one day the city would consume me too. I wondered if the itch of defiance that I'd begun to feel was my Daddy made manifest in my bones.

—

If ever there were a purgatory for transitioning souls, it can be found in the hallways of hospitals like Little Rock's University Hospital, now the University of Arkansas for Medical Sciences Medical Center.

Dante believed that Hell was created when Lucifer fell from Heaven. He hit the Earth with such force that his body created a giant crater big enough to hold all the world's hopeless sinners. Purgatory, then, is Heaven and Hell adjacent, a space created by the same cosmic event. It is neither here nor there, a way station for lost souls who've been given one last chance to square things right.

In the last week of 1986, nurses played the part of Dante's Virgil the guide for my family at the medical center. They darted in and out of Daddy's room whenever the machines fastened to his body howled. I still remember the sound of the ventilator inflating and deflating his lungs. Each time, the nurses offered up a medical prophecy for my father. "This is a good thing," or,

"This is concerning." One night, Daddy's eyes focused, blinked, and he stared hard at my mother. "This is good," the nurse said to my mother. "Your husband is showing promise. You should go home and rest." My mother didn't bother to clarify that they were divorced. She didn't bother to tell the nurse that Daddy's promises could blow hot and cold. In that pregnant silence, we were a family again. In purgatory, the past is the future is the present.

We left the building, slogging our way through an endless maze of vehicles in the hospital's parking lot to reach our car. The entire walk, the cold wind ripped through our clothes and stung our cheeks raw. Back home, my mother fed us a hot meal, prepared a bath, and rubbed Vaseline on our faces. Lying in bed, I thought about Nancy Reagan's Just Say No anti-drug campaign. A few months earlier, my sister, Cynthia, had confronted Daddy about his drug use and apparent disregard for the First Lady's campaign. "Daddy, the Devil's gonna get you for doing drugs," she told him. "Well, he ain't got me yet, has he?" he replied. At the time, I laughed. At the time, I believed Daddy would always escape death. That night, though, it seemed Daddy's immortality was being put to the test.

Around midnight, the doctor called. Daddy had taken a turn for the worse. We piled into the car and raced back up Twelfth Street. This time, Lou Gramm's shadowy voice pumped through the stereo. He sang "I Want to Know What Love Is." Knots formed in my stomach. I started to itch. How easy it was for Lou to wear his heart on his sleeve as a white man embraced for his demonstration of pulpy, soft masculinity. How easy it was for him to sing of heartache and pain as a celebrity cocooned in the favor of the public eye. Whoever he sang to, he was clearly in a position to make demands. Over and over again, he demanded to be read in on the inner sanctity of the holy of holies: love. And over and over, he insisted that "you" be the one to show him this love.

Back in purgatory, my mother assumed the role of Dante's beloved Beatrice. She was not Daddy's next of kin. She was no longer his wife. But he was the father of her children. If he had the nerve to die, then she was determined he would do it with all the dignity she could muster on his behalf. He would leave this world surrounded by those who loved him.

She emptied the contents of her pocketbook at the foot of my father's hospital bed and fished out every coin she could find. Down the hall was a pay phone. She ran to it, hands full of silver coins. For the next hour, she fed quarters, dimes, and nickels into the public telephone, calling everyone she could think of who'd want to pay their respects to Daddy. One by one, they filed into the room, even as my mother continued to make calls. Hours later, with his own personal cloud of witnesses surrounding him, the brattle of my father's life support flatlined.

—

"From that most holy wave I now returned
to Beatrice; remade, as new trees are
renewed when they bring forth new boughs, I was
pure and prepared to climb unto the stars."

—DIVINE COMEDY: Purgatorio, Dante Alighieri

—

I couldn't hum to Daddy's deafening flatline. Nurses no longer swooped in to interpret the machine's final note. No prophecies of life overcame. Instead, social workers appeared, as if on cue. They quietly made their way through the room and ushered Billy, and Cynthia, and me to the doorway. One social worker took my mother's elbow in their hand and with a gentle firmness directed her down the hallway. A different counselor herded us in the opposite direction. We entered a quiet room, and they squatted down to meet our eye level. They spoke in a soft voice. I imagine they offered us the first words of condolence we would receive about Daddy's unexpected death. Perhaps, they reminded us that my mother was also grieving. Perhaps that was the moment when my older brother, Billy, was told he would need to take on certain fatherly responsibilities, his childhood suddenly void of innocence and naivete. I don't know. I wasn't listening. Instead, I was trying on Lou's words for size, silently humming his refrain in my mind. *I wanna feel what love is. I know you can show me.*[5]

—

My first day back to school after winter break, I burst into tears in the middle of Mrs. Berdine Ready's morning math lesson. At age ten, I was old enough to feel the gravity of my father's death, but too young to explain it in words to my classmates or teacher. Instead, I cried. Mrs. Ready had read my father's obituary in the newspaper over the holidays. Without me having to say a word, she phoned my mother. Within the hour, I was home. My mother tucked me into bed, and soon I was fast asleep. I returned to school the next day. Occasionally that year, Mrs. Ready would sense that the waking world was just too much and that I needed to retreat. But most days, my mother did not have the luxury of stepping away from her job at the university to retrieve her grieving son every time he wept in class. She was still one of the few Black people in her office. She had also taken on greater responsibility over the years, including helping with organizing events for the Black Forum, a group of students and staff members that provided a voice to the college's Black community and pushed for inclusivity. She balanced the optics of her Blackness in the predominantly white office space like a tightrope artist. On the days when my mother couldn't get away, Mrs. Ready would walk in silence with me down the school hallways to the nurse's office. There, I'd rest until I'd gathered myself.

In "I Want to Know What Love Is," Lou sings that in his life there's been heartache and pain. That he doesn't know if he can face it again, but he can't stop now, having traveled so far to change his lonely life. It is not a song that a ten-year-old boy should understand as intimately as I did. But just a decade into my life on this planet, I felt I had already traveled as far as Lou.

—

Scientifically speaking, there is some merit to the phrase, "When the world gets a cold, Black people get pneumonia, and when the world gets pneumonia, Black people die."[6] Between 1984 and 1994, the social cost of crack cocaine ravaged the Black community, hitting young men hardest.

In that decade, the homicide rate for Black males ages fourteen to seventeen more than doubled, and the homicide rate for those ages eighteen to twenty-four increased nearly as much. The Black community also experienced an increase in fetal death rates, low birth weight babies, and the number of children in foster care during this period.[7] If the U.S. had invested in drug addiction treatment as we are seeing with the opioid epidemic—which has had a disproportionate impact on white suburbanites and rural areas—the lives and a wealth of potential of an entire generation of Black youth might have been saved. In 2020, the COVID-19 virus killed one out of every eight hundred Black Americans, with Black people ages thirty-five to forty-four dying at nine times the rate of white people the same age. This disparity was greatest among Black men.[8] Researchers have also pointed out that while one in five counties nationally is disproportionately Black and only represents thirty-five percent of the U.S. population, these counties accounted for nearly half of COVID-19 cases and fifty-eight percent of COVID-19 deaths as of July 2021.

As of June 2021, the COVID-19 mortality rate for Black Americans was 2.4 times as high as the rate for whites and 2.2 times as high as the rate for Asians and Latinos. And Black people are three times as likely to know someone who has died from COVID-19 than whites.[9] Inadequate health care resources in minority communities, rampant misinformation about the vaccines, and the country's sordid history of medical racism—from Dr. J. Marion Sims to the Tuskegee study—have all contributed to the racial disparities in the COVID-19 mortality rate and hampered inoculation efforts in Black and Brown communities.

I have no interest in perpetuating ill-defined half-truths about myself, about Black men. It is time we—the underserved, the poor, the disinherited—unchain ourselves from the moral relativism of the oppressor. In the words of the late American minister, theologian, and civil rights leader Howard Thurman, "A profound piece of surgery has to take place in the very psyche of the disinherited. The great stretches of barren places in the soul must be revitalized, brought to life, before they can be challenged."[10] It is time we learn to hold an individual's story gingerly alongside millions like it without it getting lost in that proverbial forest of trees.

To accept a common narrative as truth or as an indictment of the oppressed "is so 1990s." It is time we honor the individual traumas that can give birth to a dramatic potency of triumph in disinherited communities.[11]

—

Daddy was not the first Black man in my family to die young. A year earlier, in 1985, my mother's brother, Johnny, drowned in the waters of a Mississippi tributary at the age of twenty-five. Uncle Johnny was a butcher at the local Independent Grocers Alliance in Sherrill. Known for being an upstanding man of the community, he delivered groceries to our grandmother, Ella Mae, regularly. He befriended my brother, Billy, as a fatherly mentor.[12]

Johnny was a father himself, and a good one at that. One day, he took his son and wife to Sheppard Island Park near Pine Bluff to dip their toes in the Arkansas River. With headwaters derived from snowpacks in Colorado's Sawatch and Mosquito mountain ranges, the river travels almost 1,500 miles before it flows into the Mississippi River near a river port town in Arkansas's Desha County. By the time it gets to Little Rock, the river's meander belt has worked its way around the abrupt knobs, hills, and flat-topped mesas of western Arkansas. At Sheppard Island Park, the river is quite ready to swell into the flat plains and forests of the Bear State's eastern corner. Here, it flows eagerly into the expanse with the urgency of a once captive body that is finally free yet unsure of what to make of itself.

Johnny didn't know that here, in the sudden absence of familiar contours that held the river's history and spoke of its origins, the water's underbelly moved with reckless abandon. He stepped into the undertow and disappeared forever.

—

It is inaccurate to say that Johnny's accidental death was a divine act of atonement, although Ella Mae insisted on divination. Accuracy was simply a matter of perspective for my family. When the world feeds you inaccurate truths about your self-worth—and your children's self-worth, and your children's children's self-worth—you learn to exchange accuracy for autonomy over your narrative. In my brother's rewrite of this story, the tow was a hole. As a child, it was easier for him to believe a chance crack in a riverbed swallowed my uncle whole. In this version, his death was miraculous, even. Billy's version allowed my sister and I to avoid the dispiriting truth of preventable death. It masked our fear of those hidden stretches of mysterious currents that lie in wait under the surface of America's rivers.

In Ella Mae's rewrite, Johnny was taken from us because God had grown envious of our love for him. Here is where I should tell you it is not customary for families like mine, Black families of America's South, to call their grandmother by her given name. Many of our grandmothers take on the title of Madea. But Ella Mae insisted we call her by her name. She has always been and will forever be Ella Mae to her grandbabies. She is endeared to us and we to her. Which is why the morning of Johnny's funeral, Ella Mae invited all of her grandchildren into the front room of her home. Even back then, the wood floors of the house were paper thin and reflected light in places where footsteps and lin-seed oil had worn the panels smooth as marble. In the front room was one piece of furniture, a sectional sofa that Johnny bought for the rare occasions when Ella Mae would invite folks over for a sit.

I arrived at her home in Tucker dressed in my Sunday best on a Saturday, fidgety from everyone's stern bereavement. I took my seat on the couch and tugged at my starch-stiffened collar as I traced the edges of one of those shiny spots on the floor with my polished shoes. Stillness is all but impossible for the living until our dead are laid to rest. Ella Mae's voice entered the room seconds before she appeared. She was dressed in black rayon with a wool pillbox hat that women of her generation wore at funerals, black mesh pulled over their eyes. By the time she stood before us, she was already mid-sentence. It was as if she'd been filling each precious second since Johnny was pulled forever downstream with the urgent language of the Black matriarch: sacrifice.

Surely, there is no greater pain a person must bear than to bury their own child. Ella Mae buried three of eight children—Johnny and two girls lost at birth. By the time she was seven years old, she was an orphan. Later in life, she'd nurse her husband, George, through his dementia until she laid him to rest as well. That morning, she delivered the kind of inquiring soliloquy that only a grandmother who'd stared down death more than once could give.

—Do you know what it feels like to be jealous?

Yes.

—Do you know that God is a jealous God?

Yes.

—That's right. In Deuteronomy 6:15, the Bible tells us, "For the Lord your God in your midst is a jealous God—lest the anger of the Lord your God be kindled against you, and he destroy you from off the face of the earth."

It was an unusual passage to quote to grieving children, but we didn't flinch. We listened with rapt attention as Ella Mae explained that God had grown jealous of our love for Johnny. That our dependence on Johnny had subsequently diminished our faith in God's ability to provide and care for us. Pawing at the wood floor, I shuddered at the thought of God purposely removing Johnny from earth in such an ignoble way. I imagined the epic climax of the Bible's book of Exodus, the story of God's deliverance of the Israelites from slavery. In this story, God hears Moses's cry for help and divides the Red Sea, allowing the Israelites to escape the clutches of Pharaoh's army. Then, God lets the waters crash over the Israelites' enemies, pulling them to the bottom of the sea floor where I imagined their ancient bones and chariots lay.

For Ella Mae, there was no age too young to learn the power of God. Here was a mother who, come hell or high water, would ensure that her son's death was not in vain. There was no better place to teach our family's theology of love and life than on the banks of bayou baptisms and in the hours before laying to rest our dead. These were the sites of divine sacrifice.

We were children the day that Johnny drove his family to the river, but there, now seated before Ella Mae, we had grievously become little adults made vulnerable by tragedy. Ella Mae understood this distinction, even if our parents did not. We needed to learn sooner than later that desperation should one day draw us close to prayer.

—

My family is not the only Black family that preaches of a jealous God and sacrificial love. Neither is sacrificial love unique to Black people. It is a love language of the disinherited. But rather than speak in generalities, I will speak only from my own story. That way, you can believe me when I say sacrificial love is one of the purest forms of love I've both received and given. I felt this love from my mother on nights when she was not around to kiss Billy, Cynthia, and me goodnight because she was at school earning her degree in psychology. Her sacrificial love showed us that life would most certainly go on, even if her brother and our father's heartbeats didn't. I heard this love in Ella Mae's voice when she insisted that any death in our family, no matter how senseless it seemed, would always have a higher purpose than unadorned tragedy. And for years, I gave this love back to the world. I lovingly placed my time, treasures and talents on the altar of hope in exchange for the promise of a world where even against the background of Black anonymity, I might emerge luminous and particular. All it required was everything I had—my marriage, my joy, and my faith.

Sacrificial love is an unalloyed love, complete and unreserved. Yet it is born of a broken, inequitable world. Black Americans like my family have long leaned on this form of love out of necessity. We sacrifice blood, sweat, tears, time, money, labor, peace of mind, and the clothes off our backs so that our loved ones and future generations might live a fuller life than we did. We do this believing the disinherited recipients of our sacrificial love will have a fighting chance in a world designed to keep them down. In this way, sacrificial love is a symptom of oppression, not a cure for it. I see this now. After teetering on the brink of a dark depression for several years of my adult life, my well of dignity run dry, I began to perform a delicate surgery on my psyche.[13]

—

I discovered then that religion had to become real
to me. I had to know God for myself.

—MARTIN LUTHER KING JR., "Why Jesus
Called A Man A Fool (Sermon)," 1967

—

I'm not sure that Lou Gramm is pleading to God when he sings,
"I want to feel what love is, and I know you can show me." He
could be. I know I did in 1986. And I did it again in 2016.

One day that year, I woke up in the basement of my own
home. I'd made my bed in that catacomb to escape the crumbling pillars of my public life. My finances, my marriage, and
my business were in ruins. Even my mind had turned on itself.
Venerable truths passed on from the ancients to my ancestors to
me had all but collapsed beneath the weight of the tremendous
demands and very real dangers of my social circumstances. *If love
was sacrificial, then what was love when a person had nothing left
to sacrifice? Could you give so much, even if it was given from a
place of love, to the point of risking your own well-being?* Everything
about the way I thought, the entire way I was moving through the
world needed to be reordered. From the way I lowered my eyes
instinctively when I walked into a room to the assumptions I'd
been conditioned to make about Black men. Men like me. Men
like my father.

I wish I could say that the barren places of my soul were
revived before they were challenged. But they weren't. Rarely does
a Black man in America have the chance to replenish his inner

well before it runs dry. I had to hit rock bottom to understand my descent into depression. For years, I had studied racial health disparities for clients such as the Robert Wood Johnson Foundation, the nation's largest philanthropy focused on health, and the National League of Cities. I led initiatives advocating for the health of Black men. It wasn't until my own mental health suffered that I realized I'd become the subject of my own research.

What started as a quiet unfolding—late-night ponderings over warmed up cups of coffee—soon became a complete and perfect unraveling. First, it led me to my basement. Eventually, it led me to self-understanding. Along the way, I became less concerned with outward facades and more concerned with my own inner holy of holies: my well of self-love. I began to see how, in my attempts to hide my father's story, I was hiding parts of myself. In my silent critique of him, I withheld empathy. I blamed him for his addictions and poor choices, and in doing so, I failed to afford myself, my father, and men who looked like us with the dignity we deserved. With the help of a great cloud of witnesses—godsends in the form of therapists, scientists, preachers, accountants, and mentors—I began to decipher the half-truths the world wanted me to believe about myself as a Black man.[14] That sacrificial love is the bookend to the story of earth's oppressed peoples. That to achieve individuality as a Black man, I had to hide the very thing that defined the course of my life: my father's death. When you believe wholeheartedly in half-truths like this, you live half a life at best.

Systems of oppression rely on the disinherited becoming a generic people, a people of forgotten history who are severed from what Thurman calls the "logical flowering of a long development of racial experience." When I at last assembled an intellectual understanding that my father was severed from this logical flowering and bore the weight of his own unresolved trauma, I finally laid to rest my own.[15]

—

At the end of Lou's song, he issues this call: Let's talk about love.

What perfect flower of love has yet to blossom in families like mine? A love that doesn't require a sacrifice from those who have the least amount to give but instead asks that you simply come as you are. And in turn, be loved for it, and then love again. And on it goes.

—

In the wake of all that was 2020, I could feel the tides turning.

Is this what my parents felt decades ago under the bows of that plum tree in Tucker?

Is this what generations before me felt when the civil rights movement of the '50s and '60s began to crest? Did they feel an ebb of racism and the flow of racial justice?

With a cautious belief that there is a spirit at work in the hearts of both the privileged and underprivileged, I have begun to wade into the water of racial reckoning. Others like me have, too, bringing with them their own versions of atrophied resilience, racial traumas, and misbeliefs about love and survival. Ironically, there is safety in *these* numbers. As millions, we can demand that our cultures be honored. We can create sacred spaces for the individual narratives of the disinherited masses.

These are vulnerable times, and the yoke of vulnerability

is still shouldered by the underprivileged. My willingness to unearth memories that I buried long ago—the loss of my father, the heroic sacrifices of my mother—has less to do with America's shifting tides and more to do with my own internal work to revitalize the barren places in my soul.

I know now that my story—my *whole* story—is the story of a Black man in America who, as Thurman writes, is so "haunted by the dream of the restoration of a lost glory and a former greatness" that he sacrifices nearly everything in his urgent pursuit of it.

This is my story, and by virtue of that logical flowering, it is my father's story, too.

Son of Little Rock

We were running late to the Boy Scouts meeting. My father was high. His being high was not alone remarkable. Daddy was often under the influence of uppers or downers, sometimes both, depending on the day. It was more of an inconvenience at the moment. It was early in the evening, and he was driving me to my school, Fulbright Elementary, for an introductory Scouts meeting. He was taking the long way, as usual, heading west on Little Rock's Markham Street when Interstate 430 would do. Daddy often avoided interstates, saying he preferred the scenic route. My older brother, Billy, knew better. "He's just avoiding the state police cars on the highways," he explained once.

I was five years old, weeks into kindergarten, and had expressed to my parents that I was interested in joining the Boy Scouts. Because Daddy was the one who'd often take me, Billy, and my sister, Cynthia, to extracurricular school activities, he was my ride, high or not.

The drive to Fulbright was a hike. It was 1982, five years after the school had "opened its doors to serve the educational needs of families living in west Little Rock."[16] My family didn't live in west

Little Rock. Not very many did back then, save for a few white families. It was a rare corner of the city possessing more trees than people. In the late 1970s, the Little Rock School District built new schools in north and west Little Rock neighborhoods. The white families who'd taken up residence in these parts of the city in the 1970s and early 1980s were early birds. They heeded the calls of real estate agents who were steering the migration of whites to these areas. Black families like mine were directed to the south and east neighborhoods where public housing was erected.

Affluent whites made their exodus to the outskirts of Little Rock along new concrete slabs of highway, Interstate 630, and Interstate 430. The same interstates that decimated once-flourishing Black neighborhoods. It was happening in almost every American city—the Great White Flight. By 1982, the Little Rock School District was mostly Black, while the surrounding districts in Pulaski County were mostly white. Months before I started school, a group of Black parents known as the Joshua Intervenors demanded educational equity for Black students and made their demands in the form of a lawsuit. It was the start of what would become a decades-long litigation battle over desegregation in the schools, icing on the court supervision that'd been continuously in effect since 1957. The district eventually resorted to a harried system of busing. The hope was that children could, once again, be intermediaries for racial mixing. We know how it ends: Today, south of I-630, it is a poor Black city. North of I-630 and west of I-430, it is a largely white affluent city. Alana Semuels conjures a poetic image of the city's racial lines in her 2016 essay for *The Atlantic*: "The borders of Little Rock look like the head of a bird facing east; the face and beak are majority Black, while the feathers on the top of its head are mostly white."[17] These days, most children attend schools in their neighborhood, so the schools are segregated too. And those separate schools are not all equal.

Ten minutes into the drive with Daddy, Little Rock's downtown looked like Lego blocks, growing smaller and smaller in the rearview mirror as my father and I wound through the streets of Pleasant Valley. I could tell we were getting closer to Fulbright. Months into being bused north, I'd noticed the neighborhoods north of I-630 had names that spoke to the luxury of their preserved grassy knolls, natural landscapes, and the flowers cleverly planted so that color bloomed year-round. Names like Pleasant Valley, Walnut Valley, and Rainwood Cove. Where I was from, south of I-630, neighborhood names called a spade a spade— South of Asher, Pine to Woodrow. Or they spoke of lofty altruisms that contrasted sharply with life—Hope, Love, Goodwill.

I wasn't familiar with the route Daddy was taking to get to my school, but he seemed to know his way. Still, I was nervous. "Are we there yet?" I asked.

"Almost," he said. He looked over at me, his eyes glassy, receptive. "Are you nervous?" he asked, nodding his head at my fidgety legs.

"No. I just don't wanna be late."

"We're good," he said, checking the clock on the dashboard. His fingers tapped the steering wheel, his tell that we were, in fact, not good.

A few minutes later we turned down Kingsbridge Way, then into the parking lot of the school. We got out of the car, and I grabbed his hand, showing him the way to the entrance and down the long empty hallways to the cafeteria where the meeting was being held. He pushed open the door, and the metal clank of the crash bar echoed in the mostly empty mess hall. The meeting had started. Our arrival interrupted the teenage Scout who was speaking to a handful of aspiring Lions—the first stage to becoming a Scout. The cubs' parents were also in tow. Their necks craned, and a sea of white faces stared back at my father and me. Daddy held the door open for me to walk through, but I stayed put by his side, refusing to enter first. He cupped his arm around my shoulders, and we walked in together.

No one spoke; everyone gawked. You could hear our feet shuffling across the floor. I'd never cared for my father's style of dress, but at that moment I loathed it. I was already one of the few Black kids in my class, and now I was *that* Black kid. The kid whose father dressed in colorful, cutoff button-up shirts like he never left the 1970s, rocked straight shoulder-length hair, and wore sandals regardless of the time of year. I stared up at my father, suddenly aware that to most we had no business being here, suddenly aware that he knew this all along.

I shrank into the shadow of his epic self-presentation as he ushered me from behind to one of the lunch tables at the back of the group. We sat down, and the Scout picked back up with his lecture, his prepubescent voice cracking, skipping any courtesy welcome to Daddy and me. I recognized several of my classmates and could feel them rubbernecking. They were taking in all that my father and I represented to them. Perhaps they felt a sense of assurance that, as far as they were concerned, their assumptions of my home life were just as they thought them to be.

A few minutes later, the Scout wrapped up his presentation and invited the families to fill out a sign-up sheet.

"You wanna sign up?" Daddy asked.

I shook my head no.

"You sure?" he said.

I shook my head yes.

"All right, let's get out of here."

We left as awkwardly as we had arrived, disappearing through the loud cafeteria doors under the curious fixed stares of the soon-to-be white Lions.

—

One of my most enduring childhood memories of Little Rock is not of the waking world. The memory is a dream. When I was five years old, I'd often dream about a bumpy ride on the school bus. The bus driver makes a dog-legged turn, and I fly out of my seat. I tumble down the aisle, head over heels. Just before slamming into the emergency backdoor, I'd wake up.

As a Black son of Little Rock, dreaming about all that can go wrong en route to school is perhaps psychologically unoriginal, albeit inescapable. Think of the Little Rock Nine, the Black high schoolers who became proxies for America's struggle over racial power in 1957. It is the most renowned story of my hometown. By the time I started kindergarten, I'd heard numerous tales about Minnijean Brown, Elizabeth Eckford, Ernest Green, Thelma Mothershed, Melba Pattillo, Gloria Ray, Terrence Roberts, Jefferson Thomas, and Carlotta Walls. About their indelible courage in the face of militant racism. About how Gov. Orval Faubus directly challenged the federal government's authority in a way no other elected southern politician had since the Civil War. The standoff at Central High School was covered in newspapers around the world. In particular, the Soviet Union relished the black eye the now infamous photograph of Elizabeth Eckford gave the United States. In the picture, white students surround a demure Eckford, yelling epithets at her as she makes her way through the crowd to the school steps. The press praised Eckford and condemned her attackers. A white farmer named Davis Fitzhugh took out an ad in the *Arkansas Gazette*. He had Elizabeth's photograph reprinted with this message: "If you live in Arkansas, Study This Picture and Know Shame."

When people talk about Little Rock, especially in national conversations, they focus almost exclusively on the 1957 showdown at Central High, my alma mater. Most paint Little Rock as a quintessential city of America's South. Most do so because of the Little Rock Nine. And for good reason. The crisis at Central High provided the local footing necessary for the later successes of national civil rights organizations, from Montgomery to Selma.[18] The school was designated a National Historic Site forty-one years later and is operated by the National Park Service. A visitor center was constructed to manage tours and the occasional visit from prominent public figures. Like when the late Rep. John Lewis, a champion of America's civil rights movement, visited the school. I had the honor of walking him through the legendary grounds and hallways where the Black students of 1957-58 withstood violent bullying.

The Little Rock Nine crisis had the trappings of most familiar landmarks in twentieth century United States history: a white struggle to retain racial power pit against a Black struggle for equality, a celebration before the fight is won, shame, and the effects from it still lingering. Told this way, Little Rock's most well-known history fits nicely into a *Highlights for Children* magazine. Something bad happened; American values prevailed, but there is still work to be done, so help your neighbor. For over 60 years, the nine have been heralded as a symbolic, defining breakaway from the grip of Jim Crow laws. The Little Rock Nine most certainly signaled a turning point, but not just for these reasons. The standoff was a point in which America realized it would have to get creative, covert even, in its efforts to preserve white supremacy. And Little Rock offered countless examples of how to do that.

Widen the aperture, and you'll see Little Rock's complexity. The city is more than a beachhead for the rosy telling of America's civil rights movement made manifest in the bravery of children. Little Rock is a looking glass. Its story holds secrets of America's past, present, and future. Fall through it, and you will hear stories of the living and the dead, of denial and acceptance.

—

By virtue of the political and social ambiance shaping the epidemiology of a person's mental health, the story of the Little Rock Nine cast a long shadow on my childhood dreams. Put another way: It gave me nightmares.[19] The year I attended Fulbright as a kindergartner, most mornings I'd wake up in a cold sweat, having narrowly escaped a backbreaking blow against the back of the bus in my dream. For the first few minutes of waking life, the residual fear from my dream would scratch at my insides. By the time I'd make my way to the bus stop at Sixteenth and Izard, the feeling would dissipate. There, throngs of kids who looked like me would gather on the corner, waiting to be transported to the west and north sides of town where the city's plume of white feathers, as described by Semuels, stood at attention.

Beneath our playground-like clowning, me and the kids who gathered each morning at the bus stop in my Village Square neighborhood understood the impact of being separated from one another. In most other cities where busing was being implemented, Black students or their parents were given a limited list of choices of schools to attend. The school district would either approve them or not, as dictated by racial attendance patterns. Little Rock didn't do that. It made the assignments first, then allowed families to apply for transfers if they weren't satisfied. Under this plan, computer-generated "geo-codes" were assigned to children who had gone to school together for their entire lives so that they would be placed on opposite ends of town. Our fellowship at daybreak was a reminder that we had a space where we could just be, even if we were required to spend our days apart from one another in a world not ours.

Poet and essayist Hanif Abdurraqib once wrote, "Having a 'place to belong' is something that often works on a sliding scale.[20] The urgency of owning a space with people who look like you and share some of your experience increases the further against the margins you are." That intersection at Sixteenth and Izard was an urgent, supernatural convergence of ley lines, and our meeting there on the margins of downtown Little Rock was ceremonious. Sixteenth and Izard was where we daily reclaimed our joy.

—

In the 1940s and 1950s, American policymakers likened cities to human bodies. The extended metaphor implies that bodies would get sick from time to time and require cures. Bodies that fell ill from the same diseases would therefore improve from the same treatment.

Perhaps this is why the history of America's cities follows the same narrative arc from postwar years to now. It goes something like this: Soldiers return home from World War II, celebrate the end of the war through marriage and baby-making, buy refrigerators and cars, and move away from the crowded city centers and into spacious suburban houses that can accommodate their new purchases. Which requires commutes to and from the city, creating traffic, lots and lots of traffic. Which city planners deem an unhealthy attribute of any community. Which prompts planners to call for something that can carry people from the heart of the city to the rest of the body. Which becomes a nationwide cure made available by the 1944 Federal-Aid Highway Act. Which allowed city planners in the 1950s to put in roads from their city center to the rapidly growing suburbs for almost no local cost at all.

Of course, this is the whitewashed version of that arc. It does not contain red lines. The red lines that kept Black people and other disinherited communities out of certain areas.[21] The red lines that symbolized a practice of discriminatory lending that kept them out of reach of opportunities that would have allowed for equitable upward mobility. The same red lines that left Black people crowded into pocket-sized neighborhoods that city planners took to calling "slums." Slums then became the next American disease that required treatment. City planners and politicians devised a two-for-one cure: Build the highways just so, bulldoze blighted areas, and rebuild city centers. In true American form, doublespeak was employed. The cure was called "urban renewal."

By the 1960s, Little Rock was one of America's most promising patients of urban renewal treatment. Many cities sent delegates to examine its programs firsthand. The Little Rock Housing Authority employed spokesmen like prominent businessman and civic leader Raymond Rebsamen to promote the Little Rock model elsewhere. As he toured the country, Rebsamen spoke proudly of the city's urban renewal program as "a product of close cooperation between all public agencies and private organizations." He insisted that the city's emphasis on urban renewal as public investment rather than public expense was key to the program's success.[22]

Rebsamen's take on his city's recovery excluded the Black narrative. In his American tour de force, he didn't mention the unsavory side effects of urban renewal: It was destroying Little Rock's once-thriving Black commercial district, which sat directly in the path of the new highway, I-630. Known as West Ninth Street, or Little Rock's Harlem, the district was home to Dreamland Ballroom, a music hall that brought the likes of Louis Armstrong, Billie Holiday, and countless other musicians to the city. Representatives of the city's housing authority met with Black business owners on West Ninth Street, urging them to sell and pack up shop. Those that didn't budge were threatened with eminent domain. The highway was paved. By 1959, Dreamland was gone, and by the early 1980s, one more close-knit pocket of Black life in America had been decimated, an entire community destroyed for the convenience of white residents.

Had Dreamland been preserved, I'd like to imagine it being a place where my father felt alive in his own skin. A place where, in his budding youth, he could whisk my mother away to attend one of the dance hall's famous balls. I imagine them making the forty-five-minute drive north from their sleepy farm community, Tucker, Arkansas, to dance the night away on a Saturday night, arriving back home just in time for Sunday's church service. Had all the Black excellence of West Ninth Street continued to flourish, I'd like to imagine it being a place where my father felt at home.[23] From the Chat n' Chew watering hole, to the taxi hub, grocery stores, beauty parlors, and sidewalk stoops, you could take the street in for all of its glory. I'd like to imagine that on my bus rides to Fulbright, as we'd pass West Ninth Street from I-630, instead of me seeing it disappearing into the background as a forgotten, abandoned pocket of Little Rock's downtown, I'd instead strain my neck to see which Black musician's name was displayed on Dreamland's marquee. Perhaps if any of these imaginings had been reality, I would not have been required to board that bus to Fulbright. Perhaps West Ninth Street would have given my father the moxie he needed to live past the age of thirty-five. Perhaps, I would have stayed in Little Rock instead of giving up on it. One can dream, but musings like this are dangerous traps for the minds of the disinherited. In the words of theologian and civil rights activist Rev. Howard Thurman, "Rome was the great barrier to peace of mind. And Rome was everywhere."

Today, West Ninth Street is all but abandoned. Parts of the building that once housed Dreamland have been preserved and hosts a business that sells tchockies, pennants, and American flags. Walk down the street, and you can still see the mosaic tile that once marked the entrance of Chat n' Chew, now marking a vacant lot. Keep walking, and the sidewalk disappears into overgrown grass.

—

The displaced families were forced to make a way out of no way. When pockets of modernized apartments stacked side-by-side by the hundreds went up in the 1960s, the people eagerly followed.

Then came the shopping centers, schools, churches, barbershops, corner stores, stoop gatherings, funeral processions, block parties. Slowly, Black life began to rebuild in these new communities across American cities. One of those pockets was Village Square. Village Square was part of a unique urban renewal project for Philander Smith College and completed in 1964. The $2.8 million project was a collaborative effort between the historically private Black college and the Little Rock Housing Authority. College trustees formed Village Square Inc., a nonprofit agency, and oversaw the development and management of Village Square, which included five apartment buildings and a modest shopping center. In the '80s, when I lived there, the shopping center was home to the Psycolodic Snipper barbershop, where I'd sit for hours at a time, listening to elders from the community shoot the breeze and share sentimental stories from a bygone era. I met Muhammad Ali at that barbershop when the Louisville Lip passed through Little Rock en route to visit the Arkansas Department of Corrections prison in Tucker. Adjacent to the barbershop, Daisy Bates, civil rights activist, publisher of the *Arkansas State Press*, and lecturer who played a leading role in the 1957 Central High desegregation, operated an office that employed kids in the neighborhood as newspaper delivery runners. Next door was the Village Square administrative office. My mother often sent me and my brother, Billy, there with a $250 check, our monthly rent. I also have fond memories of playing with friends into the wee hours of the night in the communal Village Square courtyard where neighbors would gather on warm nights.

While these communities were erected to serve as way stations for the displaced poor until they could find their footing to move on, they became permanent homesteads for most. The infrastructure was not built to last without a consistent stream of funding to support the evolution of the communities. By the '80s, when families like mine inhabited neighborhoods like Village Square, otherwise unacceptable standards of living had become acceptable—brick walls coated in lead paint, aging plumbing, electrical fires, rusted playground equipment, broken streetlamps, cracked pavement. My mother was one of the few Village Square dwellers who found a way out for our family before the crack epidemic hollowed out the neighborhood. Before a communal hope for the future was replaced with a pervasive desperation for survival. First, my mother used a program for young adults to get her GED and an internship at the University of Arkansas at Little Rock. Next, she took a job as a receptionist in the chancellor's office at the university. Then, she attended night school to earn a degree. Along the way she saved what she could. When Daddy died, she gathered her savings and several payouts from his social security to make a deposit on a home. In 1987, months after my father's death, we moved out of Village Square and into John Barrow, a modest Black middle-class neighborhood south of I-630. By the late 1990s, the Village Square housing was demolished. Today, it is the site of modular student housing for Philander Smith College.

—

These days, I often wonder about the habits of my father. Daddy never had any illusions of assimilating to a world dictated by white norms, no matter how taxing it was to live in a perpetual state of resistance. There were times when he'd play by the rules, holding down jobs as a plumber or picking up temp positions at Little Rock's Coca-Cola warehouse and the city's sanitation department. He never stayed long. He'd become frustrated with the meager wages that paled in comparison to the hard labor. Drug dealing was a more lucrative business and offered flexible work hours that allowed him to spend time with Billy, Cynthia, and me when our mother was in night school.

As an adult and knowing what I now know about trauma and mental health, it is clear that he wrestled with his demons. He struggled to keep them on a leash, to tame them. I don't know if Daddy ever named his demons, and if he did, he certainly didn't let on about what or who had set him afire. There were hints that Daddy's father didn't do right by him, but details were never shared. When I was 30 years old, I went looking for answers, about my father, about me. I drove a long quiet road one hundred miles due east of Little Rock to find answers in a town called Forrest City from a man named Wolf. Wolf was my father's uncle. He was a living relative who could tell me about Daddy's father. I wanted to excavate stories of his home life. I needed to curate a history for myself, one that was defined by more than the broken city that raised me.

I spoke with Wolf in the front room of his modest country home. It was still morning, and sunlight poured in through the windows. His skin, made brittle from age, still hugged tight to his bones. He sank into the worn cushions of his recliner. After exchanging pleasantries about the weather and the health of various family members, I asked Wolf about my grandfather, his brother. He chose his words carefully at first, offering up a description of a calloused man who kept things close to the vest. Then, Wolf's eyes veered off to an undefined point above my head, his gaze lost in the sunlit space behind me. "Kevin, that man wasn't worth a shit," he finally said, breaking the silence.

At the end of my visit with Wolf, he asked that I join him in his backyard. He pointed to a tree with yellowed leaves. Scattered beneath it was a mound of green walnut hulls. The walnut harvest had been plenty that year, Wolf said. And the wind was generous, shaking loose the hulls, saving him the labor of plucking them from the tree's branches with a reach pole. A walnut tree can take up to seven years to produce fruit, and that's if nature's elements don't rattle its roots. This tree had a lot more life in it, he said. A lot more fruit to bear. He sent me away with a paper bag full of walnuts shucked from their green protective hulls.

I headed west toward Little Rock along the same quiet road. The whole way back, I palmed a walnut shell in one hand, resting the other on the steering wheel. The ridges of the shell seemed to map perfectly to the grooves of my palm. Occasionally, the woody shell cinched to my skin and rested in place without effort, like the needle of a compass finding the source of its pull. This land and the fruits of it would always be an extension of me, of my family. No matter if the harvest was plenty, scarce, or spoiled.

I imagined my father making a similar drive to his haven in Tucker. There he'd stay for undetermined lengths of time with his Uncle Glenn, his mother's brother. I imagined him thumbing a walnut shell or some fruit from our family's homestead along the drive, plotting his eventual break from the Arkansas earth that had both fed and tethered our ancestors. I finally understood why, as soon as my father was able to drive, he would leave his childhood home to stay with Uncle Glenn. But in truth, Daddy was never able to leave his past until he was six feet under.

The sunset was brilliant that evening as I left Forrest City, almost blinding. I drove straight into it. I'd learned everything I needed to know about my grandfather, about the emotional scars he'd left on Daddy. Any more would have been unbearable. Had my father lived to tell me the details of his adolescence, there would have at least been an offering of redemption—his life lived. I decided there was no use in digging up more from Daddy's past just to have it haunt me, even though it was tempting to read into it a new meaning from a position of hindsight. America's historians do it all the time.

I never had the chance to ask my father why he chose to take the road less traveled—rejecting white norms and defying the boundaries of law—when being a Black man in this world was hard enough. These days, I wonder if his ancestors, our ancestors, passed down a divine lure, a magnet buried deep in his gut that pulled hard to the road less traveled. Because in reality, few Black men in America get to do so without it costing them something dear—their health, their family, their sense of identity. Why travel a road that destroyed something beautiful when you can take the scenic route?

—

For years, I buried my father's story with him. I hid him like a secret, fearing I would either grow up to be just like him or not enough like him. I believed I could deny the role his trauma—our generational trauma—played in my life and that I could always keep up a facade. But even the dead need to know that someone somewhere loves them, long after they're gone. That someone loves them enough to keep sharing their story.

Little Rock has secrets too, and many are hidden in plain sight. Secrets that if anyone cared to know them, wouldn't really be secrets at all. Secrets like John Carter.[24] The story of John

Carter is not well known by white people in Little Rock because it is undocumented and has only survived through the oral tradition of the city's Black community. Black people tell his story so that he might be loved in memory. Carter's story is woven into a tapestry made up of other collectively held memories of triumphs and traumas. In this tapestry, there are parts that are threadbare, strings of stories passed down in whispers from one Black generation to the next. In recent years, efforts have been made to restore this tapestry, to document parts of American history that some would prefer be forgotten. On the sixtieth anniversary of the Little Rock Nine's desegregation, the NAACP commemorated the civil rights milestone with an educational assembly intended to shore up the racial history of Little Rock in the years leading up to it. The theme of the event was "Reflections on Progress."

—

"Our panel is based on the fact that nothing in our world happens in a vacuum. Arkansas, America, the world did not suddenly wake up in September 1957 and find an imperfect world. It was there already. There was injustice, there was inhumanity, uncivil rights, unnecessary poverty, discrimination, and inequities in everything from schools to hospitals to government jobs. . . . We have to tell the whole truth."

—SYBIL JORDAN HAMPTON, former president of the Winthrop Rockefeller Foundation and the first Black person to attend Central High for three years[25]

—

Carter's story is part of America's whole truth. Parents shared the story of his lynching with their sons and daughters as a warning for the heartless bloodshed that was possible in the apartheid system of the South. I was just a child when I first heard the story, eight years old, sitting in a barbershop chair at Psycolodic Snipper around the corner from our apartment in Village Square. The old men had a way of repeating themselves. I heard Carter's story over and over again, delivered without sentiment, always matter of fact. Always laden with sorrow. As a child, all I felt was fear.[26] The story of Carter's lynching mirrored the brutality of Emmett Till's murder, another story that was lodged deep into my psyche, having absorbed the images of Till's tortured disfigurement in Jet magazine. My mother kept the 1964 issue of Jet that contained David Jackson's photo essay of Till's funeral on our coffee table.

The story of Carter's 1927 lynching begins like so many of the stories of lynched Black men—with an angry white mob. The mob falsely accuses him of the murder of a twelve-year-old white girl. The actual murder suspects had been relocated to Texarkana, Arkansas, until their trials could occur. It was not just obvious who the real murderers were, it was judicially assumed. Still, the armed mob hangs Carter from a telephone pole. Then, they shoot him. Then, cars drag his body through the streets in downtown Little Rock, not stopping until they reach the heart of the Black community at West Ninth Street. There, a crowd of around 5,000 whites looted Black businesses and broke into First Missionary Baptist Church, dragging wooden church pews out to build a fire, setting Carter's mangled body ablaze.

You won't find Carter's story in American history textbooks. We already know many white historians don't dig for the unfiltered and raw versions of how we treat each other. Carter's whispered tragedy is another story that has suppressed the Black culture, binding social behavior and migration patterns instead to white supremacy.

"There's no way to know how many Black families left Little Rock after John Carter's lynching," said Dr. Cherisee Jones Branch, professor at Arkansas State University, in the 2018 documentary *Dreamland: Little Rock's West 9th Street*. "But we have to assume his lynching caused many to leave."

It is easy to get swept up in the shock of the archival violence of public lynchings. The brutality is boorish, animalistic, but carried out by conscious human beings acting with intention. Hold gingerly the severity of the violence so that you can pick it apart to see it for what it is: premeditated intimidation. Lynchings are meant to evoke fear. The kind of fear that travels across generations and cements itself firmly in the bodies and minds of those who can see themselves in the terrorized dead.[27] As a child, I often wondered at what point Carter's spirit left his body. At what point did his mind shut down? When did he let go of this world and withdraw into the space inside where he'd preserved his own humanity? I hoped sooner rather than later, for his sake.

Maya Angelou once wrote, "There is no greater agony than bearing an untold story inside you." Perhaps this was the demon that tugged at my father's heart and mind—a story too painful to tell but too heavy to hold inside of him. How many others like him among the disinherited believe they must carry the pain of their story alone? To escape the agony of bearing countless untold stories inside of us, Black people have had to act as both the protagonist of our own story—the hero—and the narrator. This is why as a grown man with children, I have carried forward Carter's story through my own oral tradition. I replicate the sober storytelling style of the barbers in Village Square, keeping my voice at a low and safe hum. I don't tell his story from a place of anger or fear, but from an understanding of its effects on my mind and the minds of my children, and one day their children. I could protect my kids from the anger and fear that stories like this incite, but I have no interest in perpetuating America's habit of denial.[28] Instead, I offer these stories to my children as portals to a sacred knowing: If Black people in America were not gracious and merciful people, America would look a lot different. Our hearts and minds cannot afford to carry the burden of revenge. We don't long for destruction, even if we can understand how it feels to have that kind of longing. We are, simply put, interested in redemption.

—

"The burden of being Black and the burden of being white is so heavy that it is rare in our society to experience oneself as a human being. It may be that to experience oneself as a human being is to experience one's fellows as human beings. Precisely what does it mean to experience oneself as a human being? In the first place, it means that the individual must have a sense of kinship to life that transcends and goes beyond the immediate kinship of family or the organic kinship that binds [them] ethnically or 'racially' or nationally. [They] have to feel that [they] belong to [their] total environment."

—REV. HOWARD THURMAN, *Jesus and the Disinherited*[29]

—

Carter's lynching and those of others unnamed set the stage for the 1957 racial violence in Little Rock. The brutal contrast of white muscle-flexing in the garb of a soldier's uniform next to Black children was, if anything, a tempered permutation of the city's ability for barbarous racial violence. What was new that year was the global press coverage of this anti-Black violence. Countries, especially ones of the Soviet persuasion, had good reason to report on America's civil discord and to stoke the flames. They were not exactly magnanimous motives. The Cold War coincided with the beginning of our country's civil rights movement. The two became nearly inseparable.

"Early on in the Cold War, there was recognition that the U.S. couldn't lead the world if it was seen as repressing people of color," writes Mary Dudziak, a legal historian at Emory University. Her book *Cold War Civil Rights* is the seminal work on the topic.[30]

Nothing is more American than pretending something can be a source of both patriotism and shame. *This* is what makes Little Rock so American. In America, white supremacy and the antebellum South are objects of affection and dissonance. In America, you can defecate on the floor of the U.S. Capitol building under the banner of the Confederate flag and be called a patriot but arrested for peacefully removing the symbol of hate from a flagpole.[31] Little Rock is a city that's been stretched and pulled across these kinds of opposing dualities at every layer of its existence. These layers are stretched so thin that you can peer through all of them if you choose to and see its core: denial. As author and professor Ibram X. Kendi wrote, "America is denying all of what is part of America. Actually, this denial is the essential part of America. Denial is the heartbeat of America."[32]

Gov. Orval Faubus shut down Little Rock schools September 15, 1958, a year after the Little Rock Nine started school, in a belligerent attempt to prevent integration. As though time would not push us all forward as it always has. When he finally acquiesced and opened the schools' doors in 1959, it wasn't because he had a change of heart. It was because the optics of it didn't sit well with higher-ups in Washington, D.C. The U.S. government was making an ideological play around the world, trying to convince countries to join its sphere of influence by proclaiming democracy as the new world order. Images of U.S. troops advancing against Black children, or of white cops turning fire hoses and dogs on Black protestors, were bad for international relations. As Henry Cabot Lodge, then U.S. ambassador to the UN wrote to President Eisenhower in 1957, "More than two-thirds of the world is non-white and the reactions of the representatives of these people is easy to see. I suspect that we lost several votes on the Chinese communist item because of Little Rock."

Look deep into Little Rock, and America stares back at you. On the other side of this looking glass, nothing is as it seems. Just like a reflection, everything is reversed. You run to remain stationary. You walk away from something to bring you closer to it. You call a norm an anomaly.[33] You take pride in the shameful.

When, after the January 6, 2020, insurrection in the U.S. Capitol building, our country's newly elected president, Joseph Biden Jr., says, "Let me be clear: The scenes of chaos at the Capitol do not reflect a true America," it is clear: The chaos is indeed America.

—

When my father died in 1986 of a cocaine-induced brain aneurysm, the Albrights—a white family who employed my grandparents as underpaid help—bought my family a turkey and a fruitcake. It was Christmastime, and the Albrights were known to give gifts during the holidays. The turkey was more a matter of their tradition, not so much an act of condolence. The gifts were a subtle means for the Albrights to deny their role in keeping my family under the thumb of the oppressor. Most likely, when they delivered the turkey to my grandmother, Ella Mae, they had no idea that her son-in-law had just died. And they sure as hell wouldn't have been told cocaine was involved. It wasn't the sort of thing that Ella Mae would discuss with them. Death, perhaps. So long as it was bookended with a reference to the good Lord.

When Ella Mae and my grandfather, George, married, they were wed inside the Albright's home. Their marriage certificate lists the Albrights as witnesses to the ceremony. Ella Mae attended to their home for forty years from sunrise to sundown. Each day, as she cleaned and waited on Ada Albright—Mrs. Albright to my family—my grandfather worked in the fields with her husband, Mr. Chick. Their hourly earnings were consistently and severely below the minimum wage. Early in their marriage, my grandparents lived on the Albright's land. Once George had enough money saved, he built a home on a plot seven miles up the road.

I suppose if you count all of the holiday turkeys, the hand-me-down clothes, the go-go boots and perfumes Mrs. Albright bought my mother when she was a teenager, along with the $250 they gave me my sophomore year of college to help provide support during an unpaid internship at the White House, it adds up to a wage that feels less browbeating. Just enough to keep my family grateful. Mrs. Albright and Mr. Chick considered themselves to be good stewards of the earth and their privileged place on it.

They believed they did right by my family. And since they were in a position to deem what was standard and what was exceptional, by the standards of their day, they were exceptionally generous.

If, as Mark Twain once wrote, a nation is only an individual multiplied, then multiplied, the Albrights are cogs in the American wheel. They have done their part to hold up an oppressive system, knowing and unknowingly, willing and unwillingly. At one point, it was considered generous to give a slave more than eight pounds of pork and one bushel of cornmeal in a month. Two generations later, a holiday turkey given to a poor Black family by a well-to-do white family was considered generous.

When progress is presented as a gift rather than a requirement for equity, America can pretend that progress is happening.[34]

—

Little Rock's looking glass presents gut-wrenching inquiries into America's soul. Answer the questions honestly, and this rhetorical narrative begins to weave itself together. In the words of poet and cultural critic Hanif Abdurraqib: "What are we doing to each other, and what will the world look like if we don't change?"

—

During the 1957 standoff at Central High, someone threw a brick through the window of Elizabeth Eckford's grandfather's store. Afterward, Jefferson Thomas, another of the Little Rock Nine said, "She walked with her head down, as if she wanted to make sure the floor didn't open up beneath her."[35]

I will not pretend to know the kind of courage it took for Eckford and the other eight students to walk the steps of Central High. I attended the school beginning in 1993, and I thought of them most days as I made my way through the hallways. When tracing the footsteps of your heroes, their past has a way of folding into your future, leveling the ground beneath your feet so that your steps are a little easier than theirs were. I am thankful for Eckford's diligent steps. I'd like to think they cemented a reverence for Black lives into the floors of Central High, so that when I walked them thirty-six years later, they didn't swallow me whole. Because the truth is, the early 1990s were once again a terribly violent time to be young and Black in Little Rock.

After the desegregation battles, bulldozers, and highways came the crack epidemic. What pockets of Black life remained in the city were crumbling under the duress of poverty. City officials responded to the social ills with police and prisons instead of public health and community support. In 1994, HBO covered the rising gang wars in Little Rock in a special feature called *Bangin' in Little Rock*. It was shot as a part of the series *America Undercover*. It situated Little Rock in the crossroads of two major interstates—I-630 and I-430—leading to Los Angeles and New York City, the same interstates that decades ago had driven a wedge through the city's Black core. The roads made the city a haven for drug trafficking. Territorial footprints marked by the Bloods, Crips and Folk Nation gangs grew.

America Undercover was an early form of reality TV, but it carried with it the same fittings of contemporary reality shows—glorified hardships of hurting people and an artificial dramatic irony that made viewers feel holier than thou. If it was them behind the camera, surely, they would've known better, done life differently. Outside of the small screen, it was quite simply my life. Little Rock's gang wars dominated my daily routines. This reality dictated every decision I made, what I wore, what route I took home, or what store I went to. Countless friends of mine had either been shot or beaten half to death as casualties of escalating gang conflicts or by bullies emboldened by the desperation they saw around them.[36]

During my eighth and ninth grade years, I was splintering at the edges.[37] I was flirting with street life, fading into the background of a pessimistic saga about violence in cities that started and ended with Black lives. The nightly news and HBO's *America Undercover* series told us that our toying with the streets had everything to do with boredom, even though we knew boredom was a luxury we couldn't afford. I wasn't bored or posturing for the cameras when I carried a pistol, rode in stolen cars, and got into fights. I was posturing for survival, and those were the provided symbols for it. I exuded grit and strength and lived outside of the law in exchange for being noticed. I was probably just another misunderstood young Black man to those watching me and people like me on camera, but I knew I was surviving, hovering just above the fray of one of America's undertows.

One night in the summer of 1993, I went to a party at the community pool in the Kensington neighborhood with my friends Harold and Kendrick, and a few others. During the party, someone purposely stepped on Harold's shoes. It is well documented in song and poetry that sullying someone's shoes is the ultimate sign of disrespect, even if the person isn't a sneaker head. Blood has been spilled over this venerated street attire. Your shoes are tied to your dignity, your pride.

—

"They connect man and earth. They allow you to run. That running
is freedom, accelerated heart rate by design through design."

—VIRGIL ABLOH in Lupe Fiasco's "Shoes"

—

That night, Harold's disrespected footwear was cause for retalia-
tion. A verbal altercation broke out, and the parents who'd orga-
nized the party told Harold and the rest of our crew to leave. This
did not bode well for Harold. He modestly suggested that if we
had to leave, everyone was leaving. Then, he pulled a sawed-off
12-gauge shotgun from his waist and shot up in the air, declaring
the party over for everyone. I did what anyone hoping to make
it to their next birthday would do. I ran. My friends ran, too.
Six blocks into running, sirens wailed. Cops were on our tail. As
we made an attempted dash across the baseball field at Romine
Elementary School, the boys who had shown disrespect to Harold
appeared on the other side of the diamond, guns blazing. Bullets hissed past my ear, and I threw myself to the ground. Prayer
never came easy for me, until that night. I prayed with my lips
pressed hard into the dirt, beseeching the ground to swallow me
whole, just this once. I made that timeworn promise to God, the
one that all who are disinherited make when they realize they are
stuck in the mud with no one to pull them out but not ready
to give up. I promised God that if I got home safe, I would do
everything in my power to make a good life for myself, one that
would make my mother, Billy, Cynthia, and Ella Mae proud. I'd
make it all alright.

The world looks different when you realize you want to live. That night, the storied symbols of strength and disrespect I was taught on the streets loosened their hold on me. I felt fear simmering beneath my skin. It was the same fear I felt in my dreams—fear of losing all control, afraid that I wouldn't make it to some manifest destiny. Life's turning points turn slowly, then suddenly, and I was suddenly aware that I had a second chance to pursue a future that was different from my father's. My father had resented the culture and social behavior pattern of Little Rock's southern American norms. He resisted them in his dress, in his illicit line of work, and in his addictions where he'd steal away to a surreal state of consciousness to offset the established order of his life. He was born with a narrow margin of civil guarantees and had to find some other footing to gain a sense of joy.

I, too, resented the culture and social behavior pattern of Little Rock's southern norms. But after following in the footsteps of my father's resistance during my adolescence and narrowly avoiding the judicial system, I decided I would take up a different course of action. My mind turned to the farm where my elders worked as farmhands and maids. I thought about how my Uncle Glenn, my father's uncle, spoke of the holy spirit's divine love at Daddy's funeral. He spoke knowingly and believably, offering up a dignified eulogy filled with hope. I thought about how Uncle Glenn taught me how to use the weight of my body to throw hay. Neither he nor I are large men, but he taught me how to use what I have to move bales double my size—squat, push, press, pitch. I thought about his lessons on how to properly chop cotton—shuck the wild weeds that grow up around it and take note of the good plant parts so as not to accidentally cut the cotton down before the bolls bloom. I would return to the country after the shooting incident. The country was where I found refuge. It is where I weaved together my own expression of resistance.

I started by throwing myself into manual labor, working the land, spending more hours outside than in. I chopped cotton and laid pipes in the rice field. I was up at sunrise for coffee and a hearty breakfast with Uncle Glenn, and in the fields by 7 a.m. Uncle Glenn wasn't much of a lecturer less he was standing in the pulpit as a lay minister. He modeled his beliefs and values. But some of those mornings, he would offer gentle lectures about hard work and achievement. It must have been the same lecture that his mother, my great-grandmother, had given him, my grandmother, and their siblings. When I was indoors, it was with Ella Mae. In her home, two doors down from Uncle Glenn, she fed me brown beans between work breaks. For treats, she'd make tea cakes. As I ate, she filled the silence with stories of her past to remind me that our family does not shake easily or quickly from this earth.

Mornings in the fields were especially quiet. In that stillness, I began to appreciate the natural sounds and visuals of my environment: a bird's song, dew drops on slender blades of grass and soft bolls of cotton, the way colors on the horizon changed the higher the sun grew in the sky. Cotton fields can be especially long, sometimes two to three miles long. In the thick of the summer, the cotton was as tall as I was. By the time I made it through half of the field chopping cotton, I was soaking wet. I found peace in those rows of cotton. Some days, my cousins Glenn Jr., and Curtis Ray would join me. We'd make small talk and imagine what it would be like when we grew up. One thing we knew for sure: Although we enjoyed being on the farm, we wanted a different life.

Row by row, day by day, that summer I began to question

my being, my purpose. I didn't know who or what I wanted to be, but I began to believe that a manifest destiny was within my reach. I believe Uncle Glenn and Ella Mae intuitively knew that I was shedding my shadows, embracing the light. With a pat on the back or kiss on the cheek, they'd quietly affirm my evolution. When you are so lost, sometimes all you need are those soft nudges. That summer, I altered my life's course and used my elders as my North Star. It appeared following the footsteps of our enslaved ancestors who worked the land would be step one on my path to freedom.

—

"Don't ask what the world needs, ask what makes
you come alive, and go do it. Because what the world
needs are people who have come alive."

—REV. HOWARD THURMAN, *Jesus and the Disinherited*[38]

—

After that summer working on the farm, I returned to high school with a new lease on life. I was a sophomore by this point, and my academic record was lousy. There wasn't money to hire a tutor for me to play catch-up. I did what I could with what I had—push, press, pitch. Adults and teachers took notice of my efforts. Despite my poor academic foundation, I was beginning to earn decent grades by the second semester of my sophomore year. Then, during my junior year, Tracy Steele, then the executive director of the Arkansas Martin Luther King Jr. Commission, tapped me to serve on a Junior Commission Board. Steele would later become a member of the Arkansas House of Representatives and a state senator. The junior board was composed of Arkansas high school and college students who "demonstrated strong qualities of leadership and community service."[39] I used my role on the board to help launch a nonviolence campaign at Central High, a campaign that was informed by the teachings of Dr. King and garnered the attention of Arkansas's governor and the commission's honorary chair, Daisy Bates. When Bates was three years old, her mother was killed by three white men, leaving an emotional and mental imprint. Bates transformed her trauma into a lifelong journey dedicated to ending racial injustice and shoring up the foundations of youth like me who sought the same transformation. As a student at the University of Arkansas in Fayetteville, the flagship campus of the state university system, I helped coordinate a gift of books from Mrs. Bates to the university library, including an autographed copy of *Here I Stand* by Paul Robeson. We maintained our friendship until she passed away in 1999.

Steele was the first of many guides in my life who have often appeared like unexpected apparitions, helping to lead the way or light a dim path. My guides helped me articulate my own version of resistance in civic leadership, patiently explaining the nuances of fighting for racial justice in a broken world. Each time, my guides ushered me as far as they could. Then, they offered their shoulders for me to stand on.

After Steele came Dr. Nola Holt Royster, my guide through college. Royster, a well-known supporter of education, was also the younger sister of Lottie Shackelford, the first female mayor of Little Rock. Royster was known for her passion for helping young people, especially within Arkansas's Black community, achieve their career goals. The summer before my junior year at the University of Arkansas I planned to work at a factory making baby wipes. Word around the campus was the job paid well, even if the work was menial. Like myself, most of the Black students at the university came from rural Arkansas and were not afraid of hard work. Royster intervened.

"Kevin, do you really want to make baby wipes?" she asked me over the phone one evening. She had called to ask about my summer plans.

"No, ma'am." I said. "I just need to make as much money as I can right now."

She insisted that I consider an internship in local government instead. I agreed. Royster put in a few calls with the mayor of Fayetteville and the Washington County judge, the executive officer for county government, requesting that they meet with me. After my meetings, she consulted with them behind closed doors. I do not know what was said, but the next day, Mayor Fred Hanna extended a personal invitation for me to intern for him. I accepted.

Hanna was a conservative Republican and had been mayor for seven years when I began my internship in 1999. This meant he had political clout. At the time, I was the only Black person working in Fayetteville's City Hall mayor's office. Hanna was keenly aware of this. As was I. I imagined every person who passed me in the halls and stairways there understood my presence as exceptional to their white norm. There I was, young, Black, and male, moving about the space with purpose in suit and tie and polished Oxford's. A breathing mortal that contrasted sharply with the manufactured brand of young Black males framed in mugshot stills on the nightly newsreel. I doubted that most people I passed in City Hall would make the effort to hold space in their minds for my apparent asynchronous story. I knew that my white coworkers certainly didn't. When Hanna wasn't around, most tried to exert their authority over me, whether they had it or not. It was as if any freedom I had in the workspace was a direct threat to their personage. Hanna, however, opened doors for me. He gave me access to other decision-makers and provided experiences that showed me the underbelly of southern politics: The "nice-nasty," ceremonial gestures of politeness that dressed up the dog-eat-dog world of politicians vying for power to control money and resources.[40]

Hanna was my white protector in this political haven. He would be the first of many white protectors I would come to lean on to make a successful passage from one circle to the next. These patrons of the white world have been necessary to my and other Black people's advancement into spaces designed to keep us out. But these white protectors are not angels. They play a subtle role in the collective wielding of racial power. Because their efforts fail to pull back the hood of systemic racism, progress is only a pantomime and racial equity is just an illusion. Taking ownership of reality's racist bent requires their own fall through America's damaged looking glass. Unless they execute a surgical examination of their psyche, they will never understand their personal material and psychological advantages in a racist organization of society.

My internship continued throughout the following school year. I served as a liaison for the mayor and the Yvonne Richardson Community Center. The center was named after the daughter of famed University of Arkansas Razorback men's basketball coach Nolan Richardson and still offers recreation, social, and extracurricular activities. During my time in City Hall, the center was not a part of the city's regular community planning, and the independent director who designed the programming unfortunately did not have deep educational or professional experience in youth development to design meaningful initiatives. I tried to convince Hanna to change the leadership and oversight, but he didn't want to kick up any dust and feared community pushback.

Just as I hit my stride, Hanna's gallbladder ruptured. He took a medical leave of absence to recover. With my white protector gone, the vultures swarmed. Hanna's staff cut off my access to the things that allowed me to do my job—the office car and the ability to move freely throughout City Hall and attend meetings. Hanna and I had an agreement: My schooling was my priority. Others did not see it that way and would suggest that I lacked discipline for the job. Eventually, it became too much. I bowed out of the internship my senior year of college. When I informed Hanna of what happened, he said, "I'm not surprised." I wasn't either, but I was going to need his help jumping from one white-dominated circle to the next. I informed him of my aspirations to work for Al Gore's upcoming presidential campaign. "You should make some money first," he said. "A politician with no money is not a good thing." Hanna suggested I work in the teller window at a new bank called Arvest, the Arkansas-based lender owned by the Walton family of Walmart. He was offering me a pass. But he was not offering to journey through the looking glass. I politely declined his offer. I had started to dream bigger things for myself.

My dreams, however, were beholden to the American myths of objectivity and individualism, myths that were packaged and sold as truth by white protectors like Hanna who, at best, didn't know any better than to project their white privilege onto the minds of the disinherited. Privileged ideas, like if you work hard enough and have enough initiative you can succeed in this country and emerge unshaped by a warped history or the restrictions of society. While true for white Americans, this is a deadly lie for Black and Brown Americans. Chasing a dream that is designed to be forever out of reach can break your heart and mind. Hanna invited me to believe in his white version of the American dream, that with the right (meaning, white) patronage and enough gumption, I could do anything I set my mind to. It was an enticing thought. In need of an articulate vision for myself, I embraced a patchwork identity that was presented to me by Hanna, a white man, and Tracy Steele, a Black man, who was among the first to offer me a path forward. I can't say with any certainty that they knew what was unfolding inside of me, although my mother did develop a relationship with Hanna's wife. They would talk on the phone and pray together. I suspect they prayed for me.

—

There is a wave of Black political power moving across America's South, and it has been building for some time. In 2010, Steve Benjamin became the first Black mayor of Columbia, South Carolina. His election was the ripple that caught wind and started a wave of Black Democratic mayors through southern city halls: Keisha Lance Bottoms in Atlanta; Randall Woodfin in Birmingham, Alabama; Vi Lyles in Charlotte, North Carolina; Chokwe Antar Lumumba in Jackson, Mississippi; Steven Reed in Montgomery, Alabama; and in 2019, Frank Scott Jr. in Little Rock. Before them, in the 1980s and '90s: John W. Morrow Jr. in Gainesville, Georgia; Willie B. Baker in Mount Pleasant, Tennessee; Ron

Kirk in Dallas, Texas; Floyd Adams Jr. in Savannah, Georgia; and Harvey Gantt in Charlotte. And before them, Howard N. Lee took over as mayor of Chapel Hill, North Carolina, in 1969, the first Black person elected mayor of any predominantly white city in the South since Reconstruction.

In the ocean, waves are caused by energy passing through water. Sometimes this energy takes the form of wind. Other times, it comes from the gravitational pull of the sun and moon on the earth, like a sort of cosmic kismet. In America's South, the energy that has given rise to the Black-blue mayoral wave is an old energy. It dates back decades, if not centuries.

Still, America is surprised.

The surging Black representation in mayor's offices across America's South looks powerful. But it is not true power. The power lies in the transmission of energy, from one generation of the wave to the next. If America believes that the current surge of Black mayors in the South—or the election of a Black president, for that matter—is the crest of reclaimed Black excellence, it is in for another surprise. This is only the beginning. If they are not obstructed by anything, waves have the potential to travel across an entire ocean basin.

—

When I returned to Little Rock in 2001, I did so as a fresh-faced college graduate with a bachelor's degree in political science—and with my college sweetheart, Olivia Walton. I was returning with ambitions to help uplift the Black communities where I grew up. Olivia and I met through the Black Students Association at the University of Arkansas my freshman year. As a member of the

Alpha Phi Alpha Inc. fraternity, leadership was expected. My fraternity brothers were adamant that I seek election as BSA president my freshman year. With their help, I won. I met Olivia one day when I was passing out materials for President Clinton to promote his campaign for a second term. Olivia also became an active leader in the BSA. By our sophomore year, we were seriously dating and en route to engagement.

Immediately after graduating in 2000, I joined the Al Gore presidential campaign and was appointed deputy director of the Black American outreach effort. After Gore lost, I became the director of outreach for the Arkansas Democratic Party and then accepted a position as the director of state government relations and policy development at the Mid-South Division of the American Cancer Society. At the society, I managed the public policy agenda for the six-state division. I dedicated myself to community development as president of my neighborhood association in my free time.

Olivia and I married in 2001 and bought our first home in Little Rock's Central High School neighborhood. It was a Sears, Roebuck and Co. kit house that shipped via rail in the first two decades of the twentieth century along with 75,000 other homes across the country. It was part of the department store's efforts to open homeownership to Black people who were not welcome at local banks at the time. Anyone who could afford a home with the help of Sears's lender program was welcome to purchase. This particular house had been empty for years and was owned by a prominent Black judge. At the time, it wasn't even on the market. I was committed to living in the area because it came with a storied past, namely that of the Little Rock Nine, that I thought might speak to a bright future. I spent days driving up and down the streets, looking for empty houses. Parents of one of Olivia's sorority sisters happened to live directly across from the vacant house, and one day as we were driving, we spotted them. As luck would have it, they were cousins to the owners. By week's end, we chatted, and within a few days, using a real estate template purchased at Office Depot, I made an offer on the house. We moved in a month later.

One of the unexpected gifts of that home was our next-door neighbor, Theodosha Cooper. Mrs. Cooper became a surrogate grandmother to Olivia and me. We spent hours working side by side in our respective yards. She lectured me on what it meant to be a professional Black American in a southern city. In the evenings, Olivia and I would make an extra plate of dinner and walk it next door to her. Mrs. Cooper was widely known for her work helping to make Alcoholics Anonymous programs available for Black communities. She and her husband, the late Rev. Jobe Vaughn Cooper, a prominent Black minister, were the first Blacks to purchase a home on our street. By the time we moved in, most white families had moved out.

Not many Black sons and daughters of Little Rock who went to college returned to the city that raised them. Most moved north or to the coasts where job opportunities and lifestyles matched the visions they had for themselves. Both Olivia and I were driven by the idea that everyone deserved to live in a place that inspired them to be the best version of themselves. I was ready to roll up my sleeves to offer as much heart and muscle as was necessary to promote my dreams of equality and access in Little Rock. I believed politics could be the conduit to do so. I believed, like the author and historian Robin D.G. Kelley once wrote, that I could employ surrealism not as "an aesthetic doctrine but an

international revolutionary movement concerned with the emancipation of thought."[41] I curated dreams in my mind that articulated a surrealist vision for an American city where its racial past
and present no longer shape-shifted the future. In my dreams,
Little Rock was a city without shame, and I was without anger.
These dreams didn't let me sleep, but they kept me in the fight.
As far as I was concerned, if I was fighting, one day I would find
the right series of clever maneuvers and tactics to help give Little
Rock the lift it needed to catch wind and soar.

But I was met with resistance. Many white people in my
hometown were unaccustomed to sharing power with a young
Black man. Many Black people in my hometown had a deep-
seated distrust of government, rightly so, and saw through America's hypocrisy. I'd returned to Little Rock believing I could be
a bridge between the city's unearthed racial past and its ill-defined future. I would spend a decade trying before realizing that
the more I bent and stretched myself between two extremes, the
wider and darker the chasm beneath me seemed to grow. I was
a Black American who'd become psychologically trapped in the
illusion of the dream.

———

I first met Frank Scott Jr. one Sunday in late October 2010. He
was in college. In another eight years he'd become the first elected
Black mayor of Little Rock. Frank attended the same church I
did, Greater Second Baptist Church, where we were both bap-
tized by Rev. Curtis Ridout. The Sunday we met, Pastor David
Featherstone called me to the front of the church. I was running
for a seat on the city board of directors, known as a city council in

many communities, and Election Day was just around the corner. The pastor wanted to offer a blessing.

"Kevin has the courage and the spirit to heal the fissures and the wounds of this city," he said to the congregation. "I believe that he is open to God's inspiration to help guide this city toward an era of restoration."

It was a tall order. Six years earlier, at the age of twenty-eight, I ran for office for the first time and lost. In my first run in 2004, I went up against Joan Adcock in a citywide race. Adcock was a white woman elected in 1992 and had been entrenched in local politics for over a decade when I opposed her for an at-large city director position. She has now served nearly three decades. Adcock had long been considered "a reliable vote for local residents in just about every scrap."[42] But while she's been known for aggressive involvement in City Hall business, her sympathy on minority issues is steady on the wane. She was a student at Central High during the 1957 school crisis and has been known to be cool to events commemorating the standoff. When a symbolic city board repeal of a 1957 pro-segregation resolution was introduced, she was reluctant to give it her endorsement. In my run against Adcock, I was pitted against her as "the engaging up-and-comer" "with the backing of the city's progressive political groups" going up against "the pushy old pro" "who makes things happen."

Adcock was on my mind as I stood at the front of the church with Pastor Featherstone's hand resting firmly on my shoulder. I stared out at the congregation; arms outstretched toward me in a gesture of anointed blessing. I spotted Olivia in the crowd. Her smile beamed back at me as she held our newborn daughter, Ella, in one arm, stretching her free arm up toward the ceiling to call down that holy something she knew I would need whether I won or lost. This time around I was running for a ward seat. I wanted to believe I could win a seat in 2010, even though I once again was going up against a long-in-the-tooth politician, Erma Hendrix. I believed in God's ability to work through me. I believed I could be a conduit for change. I just wasn't sure Little Rock was ready for me.

Standing there with Pastor Featherstone, I bowed my head and closed my eyes. I tried to listen to his words. I tried to receive the spirit he so urgently wished to impart upon me. But all I could think of were thorns. I'd evolved from an up-and-comer to a thorn in the sides of Little Rock's white political fathers and mothers. I wondered if Pastor Featherstone also saw this. I wondered if he could pray away the perceived pointed edges and disarm me for the sake of the ballot.

My mind drifted to four years earlier, 2006. That year, I chaired the Committee for Accountability and Equal Representation. It was a citizens' group that began a petition drive to give Little Rock's mayor more policymaking power. After losing my first run for a position on the city board in 2004, I decided to ignite change from the outside in. As the head of the committee, I petitioned for a new form of government that would give a popularly elected mayor executive leadership rather than an appointed city manager. The petition also called for the elimination of at-large city directors, who like Adcock were the white gatekeepers of the city. In their place would be a board with members who represented specific wards and those communities' needs, as well as the city's general interests. It was, in effect, a frontline defense against voter suppression. Like many cities in America's South and southwest, Little Rock had a city manager form of government that'd been adopted at the height of Jim Crow. At its inception, Little Rock's government system was pushed by groups of white businessmen who believed the city was failing to prioritize their interests. With a city manager form of government, a firewall went up between everyday Little Rock residents and their government. Special-interest groups scaled the wall, groups led by affluent white people with money and connections. Those on the fringes of society—Black, Latino, and low-income white people—became further disenfranchised, their say in the social and political shaping of their city reduced to a whisper. It was in this era of Jim Crow oppression and violence that business and civic leaders across the South found a perfect system to institutionalize racism and perpetuate inequity at the local government level. A city manager with puppet strings controlled by the white majority would ensure that city hall would work for their interests. This form of government spread like wildfire across the South, kicking off a hundred-year period of increased segregation and displacement of Black and Brown residents in cities like Little Rock.

I knew my city's history. I knew its effects on my family and me. My petition in 2006 was personal. And my run for office in 2004 and 2010 was personal. As a Black fatherless son of Little Rock, I desperately needed the city to become more than its past. I needed Little Rock to be a beacon for the rest of the South and the country. My desire for change was inspired by grief for all that could have been. I believed the disinherited people of Little Rock—people like me and my family—deserved a better life. I believed it would be inhumane if the status quo persisted. But my altruism was sorely misunderstood if not all together suspicious to Little Rock's political elite.

Pastor Featherstone finished his blessing and cued the church choir. I made my way back to my seat, and that's when I passed

Frank. He placed a hand on my shoulder, and his voice rose easily above the choir's singing. He said he was a fellow Alpha Phi Alpha fraternity brother and son of southwest Little Rock, someone who'd lived the disparities of our city but was hopeful that reform was possible through my generation of Black political leaders. He'd absorbed the classroom teachings of American politics and policy and was beginning to reconcile those lessons against a budding vision—his vision—for Little Rock. He had not fought local battles yet but would. That Sunday, he was politically untapped and brimming with optimism. The hope he saw in me, I saw in him.

Which is why when I lost my second citywide race a few weeks later, I decided to take Frank to meet a few of my supporters. I'd pushed hard against Little Rock's historic and political norms but had not done so with the finesse and strategy of a chess player. This meant that I threatened the power of those who'd rested their laurels on the old ways of the antebellum South. In doing so, I'd earned my own version of a scarlet letter. I was damaged material, but Frank was unscathed. White people liked Frank. They tolerated me. He didn't have a history of complaining to Little Rock's white leaders at community meetings about unpaved sidewalks, drugs, crime, or how gentrification disproportionately burdened Black and Brown residents.

During our informal community tour, we stopped by my high school sweetheart's mother's home, and I introduced Frank to her and her mother. I told them, "Frank is going to be our mayor one day." Frank laughed, and so did I. But I meant it.

—

In another version of my childhood bus dream, the school bus slips on the pavement as it climbs the hills of Pleasant Valley, a neighborhood on the white side of town. The bus wheels spin and screech. In the dream, the bus is top heavy and pulls away from the road, arching back like a tree being felled. I try to run to the front of the bus, but the front is now the back is now the front again. I wake up, once again, before crashing through the emergency door. I can still remember the feeling of reaching a pinnacle so near, more afraid of not reaching it than slipping and crashing from trying so hard.

I'm sure psychoanalysts Carl Jung, Sigmund Freud and Ann Faraday would have their respective descriptions of what my childhood dreams symbolized. They might decode my dream as a fear of separating from my mother or father, but their empirical interpretations of the unconscious would fail to account for my racial experiences in the waking world. You can get lost in the unconscious, especially when you're trying to avoid the obvious.[43]

But isn't it obvious? Even at five years old, Black boys in America can feel the weight of the world resting squarely on their shoulders.[44] We are children when the country makes its first demand of us: *Prove you belong here.* And since we are busy proving our worth to the world, there's little time and space to try on an identity of our own design. We are denied the chance to absorb the power that comes from staking claim in who we want to be and instead are told who to be. If we are lucky, later in life we get a second chance to eject the identity requirements foisted upon us. But by then, the stakes are higher. Choosing the wrong identity could cost you everything.

—

The second time I lost an election in Little Rock, defeat left me indisposed. I had no contingency plans for losing in 2010. I rarely do when my dreams are at stake. I prefer the risk of optimism to the sure-fire safety of pessimism. I'd given everything I had to the race while there were still mouths to feed and bills to pay. On election night in November that year, as local newscasters closed out their reporting from the polls, I kissed Olivia and the kids good night, then brewed a fresh pot of coffee. As the water percolated, I started thinking about many things. What they don't tell you about politics is that when you lose an election, you join an elite club of nostalgics—we the people, who strive fervently for the ideals of America one day and the next day are told, "Not today, small fry." There we are, all vision, no power to do anything. Like a dried-up raisin, crusted and sugared over.

As I sipped my coffee, I pulled back on my dreams, and on the nightmares, that'd haunted me as a child, then as an adolescent, and now as an adult. I pulled back on the political rhetoric and social theories I had studied at the University of Arkansas's flagship school, trying to give political and social reasons for my defeat, for the missing profusion of Black faces in leadership positions in the South. I grew impatient by the second with history's constraints on my generation of Black political enthusiasts.

I embodied the symbolic progress that America dotes on Black politicians, expressed in a collection of firsts. The first time I ran in 2004 for an at-large seat on Little Rock's city board, I was one of the few Blacks to have done so. The second time I ran six years later, I was, effectively, a political outsider.

That night, as the coffee in my cup grew cold, I accepted the dismay that settles into your heart when you realize you are ahead of your time and on the wrong side of town. My vision for Little

Rock's future would have to be a mantle for some new blood. By the summer, my family and I would migrate 1,000 miles northeast to build a new nest in the nation's capital.

—

No one expected me to leave Little Rock, but there it was: an eighteen-wheeler moving truck sitting in my driveway. It was 2011. Money was tight. Every possible expense had been budgeted, every logistical detail had been planned, down to the cost of gas to transport my family and our belongings to Washington, D.C. My mother-in-law came over the night before we planned to drive east to our new home. The kids would stay with their grandparents until we settled our housing.

My wife's aunt Angela had also flown in from Baltimore to accompany us on the drive. Angela is a professional genealogist. She prides herself in the telling and preservation of stories of Black families. The day we left, Angela told me that I had paid my dues. That me and my family deserved to leave Little Rock.

"It's time for you to leave, Kevin," she said, speaking with the wisdom of a true griot. "I see the life that you want. If you stay in Little Rock, you'll never have the stage to play that life out. Neither did your ancestors who made the same migration north and east when they realized they had reached the edges of what was possible."

I understood. You can spend your entire life with your back pressed up against the wall and never know it's there until someone tells you it's safe to step away.

A few weeks earlier, I met with Frank to tell him about my plans to move to Washington. We met at Copper Grill, a place that a friend and political supporter of mine, Mary Beth Ringgold, had just opened downtown. To this day, Frank often frequents the restaurant, and the people of Little Rock now refer to it as "Frank's place."

"I don't understand," Frank said. "You have a great life here."

It was summertime. We sat outside on the restaurant's patio while a meticulously designed landscape of palms, ivy, and flowers shaded us from the hot sun. Life did look pristine. But looks can be deceiving. Leading up to my 2010 race for a ward seat, I'd taken a job in public health policy. Nine months into my work, funding was pulled, along with my position.

"I'm tired, Frank," I said. "Everything you see that is good about my life, I've built myself. I've built it under the gaze of the public eye. I need to rest."

Frank had taken the idea of public office and run with it. He was engaged across the city's communities, serving on boards and building his political network. I assured Frank that his path would look much different than mine. I told him that he could expect to have a great life in Little Rock and a promising political future. He would be invited to the Arkansas Governor's Mansion and would be a part of the small but growing Talented Tenth who were choosing to lay roots down in southern cities. I would leave. Donned in the armor and knowledge I'd gained in Little Rock, I would move to a city that appeared less racially entrenched.

In America's looking glass, however, things are not always what they appear. The grass most certainly is not greener, even if it appears more manicured. Using your hometown as a scapegoat for all that is good or wrong in your life is risky business.[45] At the time, I believed I could outrun America's racialized past by moving to D.C. Instead, I was running straight into the belly of the beast.

Top left: Billy Dedner, Kevin's father; Little Rock, Arkansas (1978)

Top right: (from left to right) Kevin's father, Billy Dedner with Billy's brothers, Jerry and Jimmy; Little Rock, Arkansas (1978)

Right: Billy Dedner, high school graduation; Bradley, Arkansas (1969)

Left: Kevin and Uncle Glenn at
Glenn's home; Tucker, Arkansas
(2011)
Below: Ella Mae Gibson, Kevin's
maternal grandmother; Sherrill,
Arkansas (~1969)

Kevin and his three children (clockwise) Davis, Anna, and Ella; St. Michaels, Maryland (2020)

Kevin and Ella Mae; Tucker, Arkansas (2018)   Glenn Dedner, Kevin's paternal grand-uncle; Tucker, Arkansas (~1983)

Kevin (foreground) with his father; Bradley, Arkansas (~1978)

Above: Kevin (left) with his older brother Billy (right) and younger sister Cynthia (center); Little Rock, Arkansas (~1984)
Right: Kevin during his early high school years; Little Rock, Arkansas (~1991)

Kevin poses for a grade
school class picture; Little
Rock, Arkansas (~1984)

Kevin's mother poses with her three children (from left to right) Cynthia, Kevin,
and Billy; Little Rock, Arkansas (~1981)

Tills of Our Time

"And then the children open their eyes and climb out of their caskets. They dance explosively in front of the pulpit before running down the aisle and out of the church. The mourners cannot see this resurrection, for it is a fantasia."

—POET AND ESSAYIST ELIZABETH ALEXANDER,
"The Trayvon Generation" (*The New Yorker*)

The day white police officer Derek Chauvin was found guilty of murdering George Floyd, a Black man, the sun shone hot in the nation's capital. It was a Tuesday in April, but the air already smelled like summer—cut grass, honeysuckle, barbecue. The chuff of police helicopters hovering over the city in the lead-up to Chauvin's verdict added a familiar summer soundtrack. In most American cities, the choppers are a reminder that everyone beneath the mechanical birds is being watched in all their warm-weather glory. A reminder not to get too excited.[46]

But the choppers, as it turns out, were not necessary April 20, 2021. Not just because the right verdict—against all odds—was served to Chauvin, staying the feet of readied racial justice protestors. Excitement was tempered because Black America had been there before, vulnerable in our hope. It would have felt good to celebrate the victory as a slam dunk for justice. It would have felt good to believe that broad change would indeed come. But we have seen how quickly the pendulum can swing in this country from progress to regress. From hope to disempowerment. We know when to fight. We know when to rejoice quietly.

Chauvin was convicted of second-degree unintentional murder, third-degree murder, and second-degree manslaughter. These are charges that required a delicate parsing of Chauvin's questionable intent in Floyd's brutal death on May 25, 2020. They are charges that were shaped by the ham-handed tactics of dehumanizing and victim-blaming Floyd, rhetorical relics that are employed when a Black man's life hangs in Lady Justice's balance. Lest we forget, Floyd pleaded for his mother in the final minutes of his life, as he lay handcuffed on a Minneapolis, Minnesota, street, Chauvin's knee pressed to his neck. He was accused of using a fake $20 bill at a convenience store. Yet, it was Floyd's dignity that was called into question during the trial. Lest we forget, Floyd's killing was captured on video by a seventeen-year-old who had the unfortunate understanding that she was witnessing a murder. Millions around the United States and the world watched in horror. Yet, it took four days for Chauvin to be arrested.

I spent April 20 in recorded conversations on podcasts and conferences talking about Black mental health, the pandemic, and Floyd.[47] I talked about America in the wake of his killing, the quiet aftermath of summer 2020's global protests under the banner of Black Lives Matter, and the trauma of oppression. I mentioned the upticks in depression and anxiety among people of color since Floyd's murder and under the deadly thumb of the

COVID-19 pandemic.[48] For years, I have carried the water when it comes to raising awareness about racism's impact on the mental health of Black and Brown Americans. I often pull from my own story in these conversations. It is a story about how a deep depression gripped my mind, arriving slowly, then suddenly, coming in seasonal waves, triggered at one point by the acquittal of George Zimmerman, a white man, in the killing of Trayvon Martin, a Black teenager who was calmly walking down a neighborhood street.[49] The morning after Zimmerman's 2013 acquittal, I awoke with a splitting headache that lingered for weeks and a malaise that lingered for years.

The day of Chauvin's verdict, news outlets and social media streams flooded the virtual airwaves with commentary on his guilt. We were told how to feel, how to react, if at all. I must confess I was unsure of what to feel that day. I still am. Because I feel sadness where satisfaction should be.

—

For decades, the spot in Mississippi was unmarked. The spot along the shore of the Tallahatchie River where the body of fourteen-year-old Emmett Till was pulled from the water. His body was adrift for three days, tossed in the river by two white men who had kidnapped, tortured, and lynched the Black teenager.

"What they did to Emmett was so ugly that even the Tallahatchie River spewed his body back out so he could be seen and found," said Airickca Gordon-Taylor, Till's cousin, in an interview years later with *The New York Times*.[50]

Half a century after the 1955 lynching, the Black teenage boy whose death galvanized America's civil rights movement was commemorated with a memorial plaque that marked the location where his body came ashore. But months later in 2008, the plaque was pilfered and thrown into the river.[51]

A replacement was made. A new trench was excavated with rebar for reinforcement and concrete footings. Over time, the new sign was blasted with 317 bullets and shotgun pellets.

In 2018, a third sign was installed. Thirty-five days later, it, too, was riddled with bullets. A photo surfaced on Instagram depicting three white men from Ole Miss' Kappa Alpha—a fraternity that honors Confederate Gen. Robert E. Lee as its "spiritual founder"[52]—standing in front of the shot-up sign at night. In the picture, the students' smiling faces are illuminated by car headlights. One holds a shotgun, another a semiautomatic rifle. The picture received 247 likes within a day of being posted.[53]

A fourth roadside plaque has held its sacred ground since the fall of 2019. This one is made of steel. It weighs more than 500 pounds and is over an inch thick. Shortly after the sign's installation, Patrick Weems, executive director of the Emmett Till Interpretive Center said Till's family and the Center did not naively think the attempts to deface the memorial were going to end. "The manufacturers said that this is a bulletproof sign," Weems said. "We'll test that theory."[54]

—

Run these names through an internet search engine: George Floyd, Emmett Till.

Now, do it again with Trayvon Martin and Emmett Till. And again with Breonna Taylor and Emmett Till. Scroll down, or not at all, and web crawlers will resurrect headlines telling you that either Floyd, Martin or Taylor is our twenty first century Till. And then, they will tell you it is Daunte Wright. And then . . .

Ask your mother, ask your father, ask your elders: Who was the Till of their time? The Black person whose brutal killing first slashed their belief in criminal and racial justice. Shook them to their core, reminding them of the precariousness of their brother, uncle, aunt, and mother's humanity. Jarred their sense of personhood, safety, and well-being. Ask your friends, who is the Till for them? Ask yourself, who is your Till? For me, it was Trayvon Martin. For others, it was Sandra Bland, Freddie Gray, Eric Garner. Still, for others, it was Rodney King. Before King, it was Arthur McDuffie, Willie Turks, Yusef Hawkins, and Michael Griffith. After King but before Martin it was James Byrd Jr. There are more names, more stories of life transgressed. Poet and author Elizabeth Alexander wrote, "The kids got shot and the grownups got shot."[55] Which is to say that at any given point, these victims are your peers, your elders, your protectors, your babies.

When it hits home, you will ask yourself, *Where am I in this narrative?*[56] It is a question that brings the best of us to our knees. Fear creeps at the edges of your temples. Solicitude grips at your shoulders. You ask yourself more questions: *What can I do to protect myself? And those I love? What can I do to make sense of the tragedy and trauma?*

In 2013, Martin's killing, combined with his killer's acquittal, electrified America. Zimmerman, a self-appointed neighborhood vigilante, shot the teenager as he walked home from a store in a predominantly white community. Martin's parents used the amplifying echo chamber of social media to ensure their son did not go to the grave unnoticed, another Black teenager killed on a candy run. Black Lives Matter and a debate over gun laws was birthed in Martin's wake. Some called it a national awakening.

Beneath the awakening, I began to drown. Once again, the catalyst for change was the tragic death of another Black boy. The brilliance of the moment cast a long shadow, and I got lost in it. I wondered, must the illusion of progress always cost so damn much?

—

I was fifteen when a white police officer pressed my brother and me for details on which crew we banged with. He told my brother, Billy, he'd "drop his ass" if we called him dude one more time. My brother retorted, "Dude, I promise you. I'm not in a gang." I was seventeen when another white police officer pulled me and my friend Garry Rogers over for a routine traffic stop. The officer did not ask for identification, demanded I exit the vehicle, then pressed my face into asphalt with his boot. The pavement was so hot you could fry an egg on it. Or my skin.

I was forty when a dark weight of depression pressed down on my mind with the temerity of every white American that had ever shanked a Black life. I still carry the weight, though it's lighter now. Because when I was forty-two, I began a delicate and necessary surgery on my psyche. Finally, I began to press back.

—

It is easy to be Black and hopeful in America if history never repeats itself, and so it is never easy to be Black and hopeful in America. Yet, our hope springs eternal. It springs because it must.

No matter the odds, we must hope for a better world because this one won't do as is. This hope keeps you afloat most days, but it comes at a cost. Working hard—hoping hard—in a world propped up by systems that do not afford you equitable opportunities to succeed takes its toll on your mental and physical well-being. Think of the tale of John Henry.[57] Legend has it that during the 1870s construction of the Chesapeake and Ohio Railway along the Greenbrier and New rivers in West Virginia, one steel driver named John Henry could drill farther and faster than any other man. He was one of over 800 Black men who were paid pennies to move tons of rock and dirt to prepare the railroad bed. One winter, along the seven-mile bow in the Greenbrier River around Big Bend Mountain, just miles from Talcott, West Virginia, the railroad company brought in a steam drill to speed up work. For fear that man would be bested by machine, the workers rallied around John Henry, urging him to prove man's inherent value. John Henry agreed to the challenge. Using two ten-pound hammers, one in each hand, he pounded the drill so fast and so hard that he drilled a fourteen-foot hole into the rock. Legend has it that John Henry beat the steam drill. Then, he died of exhaustion.

Like most legends, there is some truth to John Henry's story. The story is based upon a real person, a Black man who was incarcerated in 1866 and leased to the railroad for twenty-five cents a day. Epidemiologist Sherman James coined the concept of John Henryism, which he defines as a "strong personality disposition to engage in high-effort coping with social and economic adversity."[58] If the disinherited's belief in a better tomorrow is a creative, unavoidable emergence from our patterned grieving of the past, then we will always take up the mantle for hope. Even when we are at risk of losing invaluable pieces of ourselves: our rest, our safety, our family, our health, our happiness.

—

"There is one overmastering problem that the socially and politically disinherited always face: Under what terms is survival possible?"

—REV. HOWARD THURMAN, *Jesus and the Disinherited*[59]

—

On July 16, 1996, I was called a n*gger by an angry mob of white people on the steps of the Arkansas State Capitol in Little Rock. As in, *What are you n*ggers doing here?* I knew why I was there but doubted they had the same assurance. I was a first-year student at the University of Arkansas at Fayetteville and was in a civic internship, interning for Gov. Jim Guy Tucker Jr. That day, I was trying to escape the chaos along with another Black intern. The seething mob of Grand Old Party constituents who hurled their epithet at us had gathered to protest Tucker's governorship.[60] They believed Tucker, a Democrat, was holding the position hostage from Mike Huckabee, a Republican. They assumed from our Black faces that we had an agenda. And that it rivaled theirs. In America, the politics of race are not autonomous. Instead, they conform to the sweeping contours of American polity. The white mob assumed our blue party affiliation based on our Black faces. Our presence was salt on their wounded egos made fragile by Tucker's hold on power. We were the nearest punching bag for their verbal blows. To escape further insult, or worse, we sought refuge at the Martin Luther King Jr. Commission office a block away.

Tucker succeeded to the governorship following Bill Clinton's resignation in 1992 to successfully run for president. Four years later, he was on the hot seat, along with several other Clinton political associates who were being investigated as part of the Whitewater real estate scandal by independent counsel Kenneth Starr. Tucker was convicted of conspiracy and one count of mail fraud, convictions that stripped him of his title and office.[61] During my summer internship, Lieutenant Governor Huckabee—next in line—prepared to be sworn in. He would be the first Republican governor to hold the reins of the southern state in over a decade. Republicans from around the country traveled to Little Rock to commemorate the transition. But hours before Huckabee's ceremony, Tucker announced he would delay his resignation. Chaos ensued. A political tit-for-tat of threats and calls for calm volleyed back and forth between Democrats and Republicans in the Capitol's hallways. Huckabee threatened impeachment if Tucker refused to leave. The crowd's chants echoed the demand. With tensions high, Tucker and his wife fled the Capitol building. Three hours later from an undisclosed destination, Tucker faxed a letter with a simple announcement: His resignation was effective at 7 p.m.

Huckabee became governor that day in 1996 when his lemmings called me out of my name. I imagine the people who slandered my friend and me returned home, in high spirits, forgetting the rage that had filled them hours before. A rage that spilled out onto our skin and onto the steps of the Capitol. For every clumsy transfer of power in America, there have always been Black and Brown bodies like mine caught in the crosshairs. A constant vigilance is required of the disinherited to ensure that we do not become the collateral damage of white America's search for her soul.

—

My son, Davis, was eleven years old when a clerk at the bodega near our home in Washington, D.C., wrongly accused him of stealing a candy bar.[62] It was 2017. Davis presented a bar of chocolate to the clerk and inquired how much it cost. When my son realized he didn't have enough money to pay for the candy, he walked to the aisle where he found it and placed it back on the shelf. As he exited, the clerk grabbed my son's book bag, spilling its contents on the floor, believing Davis stole the chocolate. At home, my son cried to his mother and me, assuming he had to convince us of his innocence. We assured him: *You have nothing to prove to us. You are our son.* I walked Davis back to the store, holding his small hand in mine. "I don't wanna go back," Davis said as we made our way north on Cedar Street to the corner store. I knew I couldn't change his mind. How do you explain to an eleven-year-old the urgency of restoration in a moment like this? The need to recoup dignity. We walked in silence, hand in hand. In the quiet, I thought about candy and corner stores, and the persistent erasure of Black boys' and girls' innocence. The same month as King's beating more than twenty-five years earlier, a store owner in South Los Angeles shot and killed a fifteen-year-old Black girl named Latasha Harlins who was accused of trying to steal orange juice. It was later discovered Harlins was clutching money to pay for the juice when she was killed. A bag of Skittles and a can of Arizona watermelon drink. That's what Martin bought at the corner store in Sanford, Florida, and was carrying the night Zimmerman shot and killed him. Hours before Till was lynched, he purchased two cents' worth of bubblegum from the Bryant Grocery store in Money, Mississippi. The details of these children's deaths—the things they were buying, the money they had in their pockets and clenched fists, where they were coming from and where they were going—are reminders of their humanity in the face of a grim fate.

Steps from the bodega, I felt my anger spilling out and tried to draw it back inside before it hatched something I could never unbirth.[63] I opened the door to the corner store, ushered my son inside, and demanded the clerk apologize to him. When the man refused, I told him to call the cops knowing full well it was a toss-up as to whether law enforcement would come to my aid or cuff me. I wasn't leaving without an apology for my son. The man issued a remorseless statement of atonement to Davis. "Never patronize his shop again," I told my son, pointing a finger at the man who'd just stolen my child's racial innocence.[64]

That same year, Davis rode the D.C. subway on his own and began moving about the world with a new freedom that suggested independence. In America, independence is costly for Black boys. The day we step out on our own is a day of reckoning. *Move like this*, the world tells us. *Hold your head up this way—not too high, now—when you enter a room. Pull your hoodie down and your pants up. Stand up straight. Step lightly. Keep a steady forward gaze and a relaxed brow.* In the words of Chance the Rapper, "Wear that fake smile like a cape. Save yourself first."

—

There was no counseling for Till's family following his tortured death in 1955. Mamie Elizabeth Till-Mobley, Till's mother, did not have a therapist to help her navigate the immense grief that comes from burying your child. Nor did she have counsel to help her process this truth: She was now the mother of an unintended martyr. Mamie pulled from her sacred well of pain to demand Till's casket be fitted with a glass top. This way, the world might see the extent to which human fear turns children into men, and men and women into demons. "I believe that the whole United States is mourning with me," she said. "If the death of my son can mean something to the other unfortunate people all over the world, then for him to have died a hero would mean more to me than for him just to have died."[65]

To invite the world into your pain as Mamie did is to invite strangers to dip from your sacred well. What was once just yours is now everyone's, and there is no guarantee that your pain will be held charitably by all. Strangers to her hallowed place of fortitude, the world mistook Mamie's pain as a superhuman strength and drank their fill of it. It is said that Mamie wept every day for her son until she passed away in 2003.

Even if Mamie had access to a therapist in wake of her son's brutal murder, there was no language of truth for Black people or the disinherited in mental health care. When Dr. Price Cobbs and Dr. William Grier wrote the first draft of *Black Rage* in 1968, the seminal book on the deep-seated anger felt by many Black Americans, it was met with resistance and skepticism by their white counterparts in the field of psychiatry. Still, the two psychiatrists decided it was not candid enough and rewrote it.

"We realized that the truth we had discovered was not being served by the way in which we were describing it," Cobbs wrote. "We needed a language that told the truth, in the way that it had been told to us by Black people everywhere."

More than fifty years later, Cobbs and Grier's clinical work to define the psychic tightrope that Black Americans walk offers a window into the disinherited's psychological continuum. But since the book's publishing, little has changed in the U.S. mental health care system. Little has been done to recognize the unique language of the oppressed and the impact of the legacy of racism on the Black community. I know this because I made the hard slog through our unequal mental health care system. I experienced firsthand the invisible barriers to well-being that exist for people of color. I experienced the effects of sitting through therapy sessions that did not hold space for my race or honor my culture. And until I found a therapist that did, I was a statistic: Black people are fifty percent more likely to drop out of therapy, even though they are twenty percent more likely to suffer from mental health problems like depression and anxiety.

—

My son was fourteen years old when a security guard followed me and him around Safeway, our local grocery store, stopping us to inspect our bags after we'd paid for our goods. None of the other predominantly white patrons were asked to verify their purchases. I let the guard know with a few choice words that he'd picked the wrong people to racially profile.

Davis says I overreact in these situations. Do I? There are some things that racism can't mature out of young Black boys.[66] Embarrassment for their seemingly cognitively distorted parents is one of them. When a child sees their mother or father set back on their heels because someone assumed the worst about them based on their skin color, the child is not yet equipped to parse shame from confusion and fear from distress. Instead, they are sorry for us. Then, they become angry because they are faced with the truth that we are not the demigods we made ourselves out to be. Finally, they are embarrassed. This is easier for them to feel. Like how Davis rolls his eyes whenever I dance. Parents who do things children find embarrassing is a hallmark of childhood. It is easier for my son to be embarrassed for me, for us, when our integrity is questioned against our Black skin. Embarrassment is easy on the knees, a lighter emotion to carry than the impossible weight of shame.

I believe my son is wise beyond his years because he has had to be.[67] Black boys in America are required to have old souls.[68] We are told that the sooner we accept our premature aging, the better our chances of survival. What happened to me when the white police officer pressed my face into the asphalt with his boot, and what happened to Davis at the corner store, was more than prejudice. Prejudice is "I don't like you." Dehumanization is "I can do things to you that I can't do to other people that are in the human family."[69] If survival of the fittest still reigns supreme, then for Black boys in America, learning to grow up fast is paramount to making it to your next birthday.

My son's mettle was tested by a man's implicit racial bias when Davis's voice was just a prepubescent squawk. Then again as a teenager by a security guard. And one day, far too soon, he will have to learn how to navigate racial microaggressions around some workplace watercooler where I will not be but wish I were. I am sure he has kept other incidents hidden from me. Just as I have my own private experiences of racial shame that gain no merit in being shared. If he's anything like his father, he has tucked these experiences away in a glass box inside his mind where he can see them, keep them safely contained. And one day, when he is ready, he can retrieve them, turn them over, and decide what parts he keeps and what parts he surrenders to his higher power. I see my son's growing wisdom, its depth. I know its sources. Being wrongfully viewed as a man when you are just a child takes something innocent and precious from you before you are ready to let it go.[70] Our learned joy from our ancestors is a relic of survival—a joy that teaches us to press back against a world that would otherwise erase our innocence before it can bloom.

Perhaps Davis already knows when I am being protective and when I am acting from my own trauma. He has sat in the therapist's office, received culturally relevant counseling, and can give back to me my pitch for revolutionizing America's mental health care system: "It is designed by white people, for white people . . ." I have yet to decipher this holy nuance of being a Black father to a Black boy in a world where white men are struggling to cope with their loss of power. I would not be surprised if Davis learns it better than I. I can only hope that he does.

—

I try to imagine what my father might have said, what he might have done if it were him on the steps of the Arkansas Capitol the day I was called out of my name a decade after he died. Or if it had been him, not me, responding to Davis's cries the day my son was wrongfully accused of stealing a chocolate bar. I wonder if he would have taken to the streets in protest of Zimmerman's acquittal or Floyd's murder. It is a hard fit to imagine my father in these spaces. I have limited stories about Daddy to project these daydreams. He died in 1986 when I was just ten years old.

Historians tell me that my father died in a decade that was often characterized as "backward." In the '80s, the country

wanted to believe that the era of racial tensions in American culture would be ending soon. We cocooned the decade in artificial
symbols of progress, like the then-controversial bill that made the
Rev. Martin Luther King Jr. Day the first new federal holiday
since the 1940s and the first to honor a Black man. This, set to
the backdrop of the Miami race riots. The riots occurred after the
acquittal of four police officers who beat a motorcyclist to death
and initially said he died in a crash. Images of cities in flames
had not been seen since the late '60s.[71] Ruthless murders like the
killing of innocent Chinese American Vincent Chin in Detroit in
1982 revived images of racially motivated barbarous murders that
haunted Americans for years.[72] People say the '80s were a pream-
ble to the hate crimes and racial unrest that plagued the following
decade. Perhaps it was this digression that made my father's skin
prickle with phantom pains and his mind fill with angst. Perhaps
the ebb and flow of justice in 1980s America was a current too
strong for him. Along the way, he lost his footing and fell into
addiction. Then, his addictions swept him away. Hoping while
carrying the weight of generational trauma is all but impossible if
you are not given time and a safe space to set that boulder down.
My father refused to scale the edifice of hope while such a heavy
burden rested on his heart and mind. He bucked Sisyphus's curse
and let the rock roll. I do remember Daddy's essence: "Live fast,
die young." If he lived fast and died in a backward decade, then
can you really blame him for feeling like he was going nowhere,
resolved to resist and escape the reality around him?

    In his book *Jesus and the Disinherited*, Rev. Howard Thurman
outlines three forms of resistance for the disinherited: conscious
assimilation, reduced contact, and an outward defiance that starts
in the mind.[73] My father never had any allusions of assimilating.

Neither was he one to temper his presence, be it through his flamboyant style of dress or his refusal to recoil in a room where he was the only Black man and all eyes were on him. His defiance was embodied in his misunderstood swag and subsequent quiet middle finger to the world. Daddy's defiance started in his mind, but his mind never had a chance to heal. In the words of Thurman, he "could not deal with the question of his practical life, his vocation, his place in society" because he had not first "settled deep within himself this critical issue" of his life's meaning in a world that had wronged him so deeply.

My father's outward form of resistance stands in sharp contrast to the matriarch of my maternal family—Ella Mae. Under an unassuming plan of nonresistance, my grandmother took up the position of imitation. Ella Mae was a maid her entire life to one of the ten white families who owned most of the farmland in Sherrill, Arkansas. She maintained an uncanny relationship—she would even call it a friendship—with Ada Albright, the white woman of the house who she tended to, up until Mrs. Albright's death. It is tempting to sit with Ella Mae over a cup of tea and one of her famous pies and pick apart the nuance of her befriending a family with the legacy of slave-owning in the antebellum South. I have not had this conversation with her but could. She is still alive at the time of this writing in July 2021. She is 104 years old.

Thurman would say that the aim of her disposition in the world is to assimilate to the prevailing systems and social behavior patterns of the dominant group. In this case, white supremacy. By yielding herself to that which, deep within, she recognizes as being unworthy, she is negotiating a strategic, albeit unfortunate, loss of self. For this reason, I cannot in good conscience ask Ella

Mae to defend her rationale for reducing all outer signs of resistance to her oppressors. Doing so could unearth an unspoken knowledge of what Ella Mae, and so many Black matriarchs, had to sacrifice so that her children and grandchildren might one day outwardly resist the great barriers to freedom. "It's why we laugh at the stories of the grandmother who takes no shit, but we know not to laugh too long," writes poet Hanif Abdurraqib.[74]

Ella Mae's younger brother, Willie Calhoun, took up Thurman's "reduce contact" strategy of resistance. He often said things that alluded to his resentment of his sister's "relationship with white folk." He made it clear that he had no interest in working on the farm or cleaning for them. He migrated north, settling in Chicago, along with a host of other Black migrants from the South. In the latter years of his life, after suffering from a stroke, Uncle Willie came to live with my grandmother. Ella Mae couldn't stand the idea of her baby brother living out his final years in a nursing home. After all, it is those who have their backs against the wall who can show the world the way out of antipathy and back to love.

—

Mamie Elizabeth Till-Mobley, Emmett Till's mother, Chicago, summer 1955:

> "I realized this wasn't a fight that I could do. That it was going to be a fight that we had to do. That the people would do for me. I want you all to stand by me because it's going to be a fight. If you stand by me, I will stand by you because I am not afraid."[75]

Sybrina Fulton, Trayvon Martin's mother, Portland, Oregon, April 14, 2015:

"Like any other mother I cried many tears. One day, when I started to cry, I was on the floor. When I opened my hands, I saw I had nothing but tears in my palms. I told myself, 'You can do better than this. You can do more than just cry.' And so, I decided in that moment that I had to do more, that I had to be the voice for my son. . . . There's something you can do as well. Make sure that you're lending your voice. Make sure that you're lending your talent. Because if you really want to make a difference, that change will start with you."[76]

—

Years later, I cannot recall if it was a Twix or a Hershey's candy bar that my son wanted from the store the day he was assumed a thief because of the color of his skin.[77] Trivial at first blush, these patterned details are like shrapnel in the minds of the disinherited, fragments of traumatic memories recorded and encoded—a snapshot of a candy wrapper, the feeling of blood rushing from the gut to your muscles, a mental video gone viral with a soundtrack that leaves you breathless. Malicious fragments like these, if not dealt with, are known to manifest as physical expressions of affliction. Unconsciously, we hold onto them. We lose sleep. We get angry, sad, despondent, and we don't know why. We fall ill. Like a virus, these raw traumatic memories become sticking points that cause our mental and physical processes to malfunction.[78]

After a New York City police officer put Eric Garner in a prohibited chokehold, killing him, I promised myself that I would never watch videos of police brutality or anti-Black violence. This has been a difficult promise to keep and a challenging self-protective habit to teach. Especially as a father of three Black children who are growing up in a world that serves up viral content on glass screens when they're under the covers at night, distant from me. I encourage them to do the same, to look away. But I cannot control how they choose to protect their minds. I can only tell them that it is imperative to do so. That enough events will require them to understand the complexities of their race and that those events will likely be painful. And that they are not alone in whatever feelings those events trigger.

—

In 2019, days after the picture of the Ole Miss students holding up their guns in front of Till's marred sign appeared on social media, the University of Mississippi at Oxford police reported the image to the Federal Bureau of Investigation. The bureau declined to investigate, saying the photo did not pose a specific threat. The Justice Department's Civil Rights Division said they *may* investigate, but never did. And Ole Miss's then-spokesman, Rod Guajardo, said the image was not in violation of the university's code of conduct. The gun-toting Ole Miss boys suffered little to no consequences.[79]

One year earlier, the Justice Department had reopened the investigation into Till's brutal murder.[80] Carolyn Bryant Donham, the former wife of one of the alleged murderers, recanted her 1955 trial testimony in the book, *The Blood of Emmett Till* by Timothy Tyson. In the 2017 book, Bryant Donham said that her testimony in court, of Till grabbing her and making sexual advances, was not true. She also said, "Nothing that boy did could ever justify what happened to him." It took Bryant Donham over 60 years to come to terms with her conscience enough to offer back a thin veneer of humanity to Till. Who's to say if her delayed remorse was offered up as recompense for Till's precious life or her own eternal salvation? Who's to say if she performed a surgery of her own psyche to arrive at the truth of Till's death and her part in it?

A National Public Radio investigation published in early 2021 found that since 2015, police officers have fatally shot at least 135 unarmed Black men and women nationwide. The killings have led to almost thirty judgments and settlements totaling more than $142 million, records show. Dozens of lawsuits and claims are pending. Chauvin is just one of these unrestrained officers. In all of his privileged imperfections, he played the part of a perfect scapegoat, symbolizing what it might look like to right our flawed systems in the name of racial justice. But Chauvin's guilt does not cleanse America from her racial sins. One reckless cop was removed from the streets. But it won't shock a system that is cemented in policies and practices that teach its enforcers to fear dark bodies like my own.

If racial justice were a destination—a single verdict, a sentence served, a case reopened—America would have arrived countless times by now. But these are not acts of justice. America's soul, the future of Black people, and racial equity does not—cannot—hang in the balance of one white man's guilty verdict, or one white woman's deferred admission of truth. The oppressors cannot be both the knee that presses the disinherited into the earth and the symbolic handmaidens of freedom. These legal and civic milestones are points of accountability *en route* to justice.

The path winds through harried litigation battles that inform new anti-racist policies. It is paved by the blood and sweat of protestors, and by the screams of mothers and fathers who buried their children, many of them killed by bullets in their backs.

The camber of racial justice in America has always leaned heavily on the stories of each generation and what each generation is willing to do in the backbreaking fight against racist misbeliefs and policy. In the words of Ibram X. Kendi:

> "Racial history does not repeat harmlessly. Instead, its devastation multiples when generation after generation repeats the same failed strategies and solutions and ideologies, rather than burying past failures in the caskets of past generations."[81]

So long as we believe justice is a destination, rather than a journey, the jubilee of justice will always feel "just past the horizon."

—

Before the Tills of our time become symbolic points of accountability en route to justice, they are sons, daughters, wives, husbands, fathers, mothers, uncles, aunts, friends, coworkers, babysitters, godparents, children of God. Their humanity, the violation of it and the fight to redeem it, is the provocation for change. The indignities of the Tills of our time often require the disinherited to make harrowing journeys through their psyches. They are tests of our spiritual backbone. At the individual level, the journey requires a surgical examination of why you think the way you think. An unpacking of the cognitive distortions that repeated traumatic events near and far to you have caused.[82] My psychic journey was long and arduous, but it is what brought me out of the dark. These days, I keep myself in the light by illuminating the path to joy that I discovered. This way, others may follow.

As a collective, we must keep the vigils, the protests and the political battlefields occupied so that the Tills of our time are always remembered by name, not just by symbol. Ahmaud Arbery, George Floyd, Eric Garner, Freddie Gray, Trayvon Martin, Breonna Taylor, Daunte Wright. Their humanity remembered is accountability for America's labored journey toward justice. In the words of James Baldwin, "Experience that destroys innocence also leads one back to it."

—

In my living room hangs a painting by Washington, D.C., artist Timoteo Murphy. The canvas is a piece of untreated pinewood that measures four feet by four feet. There are areas of the painting where the wood shows through and splinters. In one corner is a charcoal sketch of Trayvon Martin. In the other, Michael Brown. Nestled between the two profiles are two doves. When I purchased the piece, I asked Murphy to describe the energy he painted with. I wanted to know the emotions behind his brush strokes and pencil marks. Was it anguish? Anger? Hope? "All of it," he said. "I felt it all."

I purchased the painting in August 2020. Later that year, around Thanksgiving, I was reading the book of Luke, chapter two. It's the chapter that details Mary and Joseph's struggle to find a proper setting for the birth of Jesus. A particular verse stood out to me, Luke 2:24: "And to offer a sacrifice in keeping with what is said in the Law of the Lord: 'a pair of doves or two young pigeons.'" *What was it about the two doves?* I found a biblical commentary that cross-referenced the text with scripture from the Old Testament book of Leviticus. The Old Testament scripture stipulated sacrificial allowances for the disinherited. If one could not afford a lamb to make a burnt offering to atone for sins, doves or pigeons were acceptable. Mary and Joseph were dirt poor, had left the only home they knew, fated for a life that would make them parents of an enemy of the state. To consecrate the birth of their son, they offered what they had: two doves. After discovering that passage, I could not help but think about how the deaths of Martin and Brown launched a movement. The symbolism of them as sacrifices is akin to the doves in the biblical story. At the time of their deaths, America was in desperate need of restoration, which could only begin with the acknowledgement of her racial past and genuine soul search to address it.

As I write this, summer wanes. The one-year anniversary of George Floyd's death has come and gone. Each night, the evening news tells us that crime is once again spiking, this time instigated by a perpetual angst over a pandemic that just won't end. And each night, police choppers circle the skies of American cities. If you, too, like me, are conflicted in your feelings about Chauvin's legal fate, about the future, know that there is truth and power in the complexity of your emotions. On this sanctified journey to justice, know this: We can reclaim a steadfast joy from within, even if the world around us lacks luster. We can rejoice for the moments of accountability that are birthed from verdicts, protests, and cracks in long-held racist systems. And we can be quietly apprehensive about our fragile hope for even greater change.

Every Conscious Black Man
Needs to be in Therapy

"The test of life is often found in the amount of pain
we can absorb without spoiling our joy."

—HOWARD THURMAN, a note inscribed in his 1955
volume on spirituals, *Deep River*, addressed to Dr. Martin
Luther King Jr. and Coretta Scott King

It's close to midnight on July 13, 2013, the night of George
Zimmerman's acquittal, and I have nothing left to give the
day. I've just returned to my home in Brookland, a neighborhood in the northeast corner of Washington, D.C. I've concluded
that there is little I can do in my waking life that will make me
feel better about how the last hour has unfolded. It has otherwise been a good day—a warm Saturday evening spent enjoying
the city's bar scene with a few friends, blowing off steam from a
long workweek. Our conversations were lighthearted, a distrac-
tion from an otherwise listless anticipation of bad news, which I
quietly hoped would be good. After three weeks of testimony and
two days of jury deliberations, Zimmerman's impending verdict
is taking up residence in my daily musings. It is making itself

physically manifest in my clenched jaw and tense shoulders.[83] Zimmerman, a self-deputized gun owner and neighborhood watch coordinator for his Sanford, Florida, gated community, has been charged with the murder of Trayvon Martin, an unarmed Black seventeen-year-old who was walking along the street.

Earlier, as my friends and I bid adieu for the evening, one hundred protestors gathered eight hundred miles away outside the courthouse in Sanford where Zimmerman's case is being heard.[84] What started as a routine homicide case in the small town is now a national civil rights cause scrutinizing racial profiling, lax gun laws, and their tragic consequences. Now home, I turn on the television and read a ticker crawling across the bottom of the screen: "Zimmerman is acquitted in Trayvon Martin killing." It is 10:30 p.m., and Zimmerman is found not guilty of second-degree murder.

Zimmerman fatally shot Martin on the night of February 26, 2012. I spent the last year leading up to his trial and tonight's verdict in a state of risky optimism. I wanted to believe the outcome of Zimmerman's trial would be fair. Even though Sanford's police initially decided not to arrest him until the public outcry had reached a fever pitch six weeks after Martin's death. It was a cry that was first sounded by Martin's parents, Tracy Martin and Sybrina Fulton. I wanted to believe there would be justice for all of them. Even though five months before Martin was killed, the Sanford police distributed fliers at a neighborhood watch meeting that read, "Know your neighbor" and issued advice on how to profile a neighborhood block. I wanted to believe that Zimmerman's trial would bring forth objective truth to offer closure to a nation that was once again shaken to its bones by another senseless death of a Black boy who had done nothing wrong. Even though email correspondence between Zimmerman and the Sanford police department showed a cordial and anything-but-objective relationship.[85] I had been holding space in my consciousness for the ideals to which America so proudly claims to anchor itself. Ideals like democracy, justice, and the pursuit of happiness, even though the country has yet to make good on these promises for the Black community. But tonight, standing in my living room with pictures of my ancestors staring back at me, watching the ticker tape scroll across the television, it seems my beliefs have soured.

—

It was either 2013 or 2014 when things began to unravel. I can't be sure. And it's hard to say when the chokes finally came off, when I was cut from my loom of dolor. Maybe it was 2017. Then again, it could have been a start-stop sort of thing. Sleeping in the basement of my home for weeks at a time. Skipping breakfast and lunch, opting for bed until two in the afternoon. Recouping my sense of self for a few months. Until I slipped, once again, down the rabbit hole and into the subterranean levels of my mind, and subsequently my home. One is never sure of past details when that past is clouded by depression.[86]

I've traced my journal entries and calendar back to those years to timeline this dim period of my life. It is an honest pursuit, memorializing the gaps in my story that were lost to a heaviness of the heart. June 26, 2015, reads: *Central High School Class Reunion, Little Rock, Arkansas.* October 10, 2015: *Million Man March, Washington, D.C.* Though, in truth, I opted for a solo horseback ride at Piscataway Riding Stables in a nearby Maryland suburb instead of gathering with the masses on the steps of the United States Capitol. By then, I was retreating into the recesses of my mind. In fall 2015, the colorful blocks on my calendar noting work meetings and life events become fewer and farther between, reading less like a game of Tetris and looking more like a void of white space.

It all happened slowly, then suddenly. First, my uprooting from Little Rock, Arkansas. Then, the subsequent deferment of my dreams—visions for a new kind of American South, which I believed I'd inherited and was supposed to make good on for the sake of the disinherited people of my hometown. People like me. Then, gradually, my feverish drive to build a new life for my family in the nation's capital began to wane. The carriage of my movements and maneuvering of my life's responsibilities were marked by an ungainly gracelessness. I missed work appointments, I forgot my kids' birthdays, and I made excuses to leave home to disappear into the aisles of grocery stores. I lost interest in our house renovations. Funding was pulled for the childhood obesity program I was supporting. Then, more work dried up.[87] I was nickeled and dimed in what little contracting work I could salvage, paid the lowest among my predominantly white coworkers even though I often had the most experience. I was losing steam in that fight too. Self-advocating for higher pay left me winded and still broke. I applied for jobs, attended interviews, and each time was turned away. During all of this, my youngest child was born. The weft in the tapestry of my meticulously woven life had loosened. The thread was unraveling. Until suddenly, there I was, sleeping in the guest bed in the dimly lit underbelly of my own home, undone.

In one particular basement memory, my bare feet rest flat on the floor. It is 2014. I am sitting on the bed, reaching down, pressing a finger into the soft tissue between my toes. I am making sure it is me in my body and not some stray waif from a dream. The bed is made, though I can't remember if I made it or simply slept on top of the covers. It is morning; I know that much. Sunlight pours in through the hopper window above the bed. This wasn't the first morning I'd awakened in the basement in a trance. I cradle my head in my hands until my eyes adjust to the daylight. I need coffee, I need my senses to come online. I hear my children's feet shuffling across the floor above me, my wife, Olivia, beckoning them out the door to school, echoes from the waking world. I spool a loose thread from the bed's comforter around my finger and snap it loose. The fabric puckers, frays. Another strand emerges. It, too, is unraveling. I stand up, make my way to the stairs, and begin my climb. I stop and grip the railing, pausing on the steps until the noises above me fade. The sound of Olivia and the kids' chatter grows distant as they make their way out of the house. The front door slams shut, and I resume my climb, opening the door at the top of the basement stairwell to an eerie silence. At least the basement's quiet matches its refuge. Above ground, the lacuna of life is disquieting, misplaced. I think to turn back, to return to the underground, but the front door opens. It is my middle child, Ella. She runs through the parlor to the kitchen. I wonder if she sees me standing in the frame of the basement door. "Do you know where my lunch bag is, Daddy?" Ella yells. I am not a ghost after all. My heart races. How can I possibly know where her lunch bag is if I am not even sure whether I am awake or dreaming, a spook or flesh and blood?[88] I walk into the kitchen. Ella is nowhere to be seen, but the refrigerator door is ajar. "Ella, how many times do I have to tell you to close the refrigerator door?" I slam it shut, and the sound of glass shattering follows the thud of the door. Ella peeks around the corner of the pantry room doorway. Her eyes beam. "I found it," she says quietly. She holds her bag up, a peace offering. "I left it in the other room, accidentally." I drag my hand across my head, resting it on my neck. "OK, good," I say, offering up all of the softness of voice I can muster. "Go on now, before you're late to school." She disappears from the doorway and runs out the front door, slamming it with the same insolence and brass as I'd shown the refrigerator door. *Like father, like daughter*, I think, then wince at the thought of her one day sharing my current state of despondency, my anger. *Please, Lord, don't let her know this unease.*

—

2014 JOURNAL ENTRY

"God, I don't know what you are up to, but I trust you. It's been difficult for me, but I'm trusting you. I'm available for your service and work. I no longer have a destination."

—

During my depression, there were times when I thought, "It wouldn't be so bad if I got hit by a bus." Depression often brings with it thoughts of suicide or death, even if there is no intent to take one's life. Some days, I would imagine colorful and detailed scenarios in which my provoked, albeit accidental death, might afford my children and Olivia with insurance money to elevate their standard of living. I learned the nuances of being a financial beneficiary to someone's death when Daddy died. My father did not have an insurance policy, but my mother was able to recoup some financial assistance from his social security. My musings also accounted for the cultural taboos of suicide within the Black community. In the Black church, you can find help for just about everything but suicide prevention. It is considered a sin to take your own life. I did not want to go to hell, even though I believed my death had a silver lining. My daydreams of death would go something like this: I'd imagine myself being robbed and refusing to give the robber my goods. In our tussle, my words and posture would become larger than life, intimidating the robber. He would stand down. He would think he'd met his match. Ever since I was a young boy, I have welcomed opportunities to take my stand against bullies. In these confrontations—be it reality or in my daydreams—my aim is to survive. But if I don't, my eulogy would be respectable. In this way, I would evade suicide, though elegantly leave the earth with my honor and salvation intact.

While pinpointing the start of my adult depression feels like a wild goose chase, I can easily point to when the seed of hope for a better life was planted. By the time I enrolled as a first year at the University of Arkansas at Fayetteville, my mind had been cultivated, made ready for big dreams. I'd pieced together as much information as I could to decide what my path to a better life would look like. At the university, I articulated those dreams. Young Black men in America are often stitching together pieces of selfdom, pulling from the best examples around us. In this way, we are patchworks of brilliance, no matter how threadbare. In my case, there were few men I truly admired growing up. Addiction took hold of my father early in his adult years. By the time I was ten years old, he was six feet under. It would take decades before I redeemed parts of Daddy to complete my patchwork. I looked to my Uncle Glenn, a humble but sturdy soul who worked the street life out of me one summer on a farm. He taught me to shuck peas, chop cotton, and how to buck the noise of the world when it all becomes too much—drown it out with joyful song at a Sunday church service in polished loafers.[89] I looked to my older brother, Billy, who took on parental responsibilities as a child after our father died and then in my adult years made himself available daily for my phone calls when I needed to hear a reassuring and familiar voice. I looked to Tracy Steele, a former Democratic member of the Arkansas House of Representatives and the first Black professional man who took an interest in me. I met him as a teenager shortly after giving up on street life while unsure of how to escape the trying fate of Little Rock's blighted neighborhoods. Tracy offered me an alternative: become an elected official; help fix the world around you so that it mirrors your freedom dreams. He was the people's champ, loved for the respect he gave others and showed himself. His was a refined voice in a dog-eat-dog political power structure. I wanted to be like that. I wanted to help create a better life for others. When you come from a world of not having much and then you are exposed to the good life, every decision you make thereafter is based on never going back. Or better yet, forever moving forward. It becomes the superior motive for your existence: creating a better life, now and in the future, for yourself, your friends, your partner, your kids, the family you left back in Little Rock, their community, your new community in D.C. Until one day, you find yourself trying to boil the ocean with a flint and nest of tinder. You burn yourself in the process, and the ocean stays cold.

—

2015 JOURNAL ENTRY

"It has been a long time since I have been truly happy. But it feels like I'm on the verge of life coming together again. I have been doing lots of internal work. I have been praying. Sometimes it doesn't feel like God is there. But I have to believe that I am heard."

—

Now it is another warm Saturday in D.C. It is 2015. I am folding white linen napkins, occasionally trimming a loose thread that's untangled itself from serge edges. I shift my attention to flower arrangements and fidget with the placement of each vase. Next, I negotiate with a caterer I have hired about the desserts she's selected and whether they appropriately complement the evening's soul food theme. The cook is here, in my home, to help me cater to an eclectic and impressive guest list. It is a list I have curated, pulling from my expanding network of political heavyweights and budding socialites in the Capitol. This is one of many parties I host in the years of my unraveling. This time, it is in honor of my dear friend Rashod Ollison, a Little Rock native and journalist. He has just published his first book. It will be his last, though none of us know that now. None of us know that three years later, cancer will take him from us all too soon. The guests will be arriving shortly. Each of them knows me, but they do not know that I am on the verge of losing almost everything I have, materially and spiritually.

—

As I look back, I know now that I was building a house of cards. Up and up, stacking each symbol of prestige atop another—a dinner party here, a coveted consulting contract there—failing to see the hollowed foundation upon which I was building: a prescribed sense of self. Until it all came crashing down. I have spent many years of my life, like Ralph Ellison's Narrator in *The Invisible Man*, burning parts of my personhood to see in the dark. I masked inherent character traits when they made a white coworker or investor feel uncomfortable. I attempted to define myself through the values and expectations that the world, which constantly misunderstood me, imposed on me. To be misunderstood, to relinquish old identities to build new ones, is not a unique human experience. Each of us can attest to a time of identity foreclosure, a period in which we relinquish the mystique of our learned personality and disposition. We re-evaluate. We examine the whys and hows of who we are. We narrate our origin stories and edit with hindsight the parts that once eluded us.

But for the disinherited, choosing what to become is not inevitable. In fact, it often feels like an illusion, out of reach. When racism is an obstacle to your development, this evolution is delayed, and in some cases missed altogether. I have turned many heads at dinner parties when I've offered up my unfiltered version of this observation: Black people often don't know who they are. Like adolescents, we have had to take on expectations of how we should behave, how we should talk, how we should resist, and how we should heal. In exchange for a gutted and highly stipulated acceptance into the American fold, we commit to these prescribed identities with fervor.[90] Yet we, the disinherited, are not given an equitable stake in this exploration of self. The roles and archetypes we are assigned limit our complexities as individuals.

We are forced to play inauthentic parts. We are told on the one hand that we must work hard to achieve our dreams. Yet in some spaces, we are told that certain careers, institutions, and positions are not for us.

One day, after carefully constructing my house of cards, having committed everything I had to an articulately designed life, the wind blew just so, and there I was, scattered and false in my sense of self. The beauty of being scattered to the wind is that with the cards laid out before me, one by one I could decide what was me and what was not. I let go of identities prescribed to me.[91] I began to explore new identities. I became a truer version of the Black man I wanted to be.

—

2016 JOURNAL ENTRY

"I now understand that I am on a journey, and I am grateful for the growth. Lord, help me to discover more lessons within my experiences. Please use me in your service. Help me to discover my authentic self. Remove all ego from me. Help me to operate in my highest self."

—

There have been many attempts to prescribe the right way to be a Black man in America. Walk from room to room in my home, and images of my ancestors hanging from the walls will tell you the story of how the men in my family went about it. Some of my grandfathers pose stoically next to equally reticent grandmothers, their industry showing through in the details of their attire and in the backdrop of their homestead on a farm. These are the ancestors who worked as sharecroppers and paid help in the ante-bellum and postbellum South, maintaining a simple and lonely life, limiting their interactions with white people, or any people for that matter. Some ancestors offer the camera a forced smile, most likely after a long day's work in which they adopted the manners and speech of whites, assimilating under a manufactured guise of belonging. And others, like my father, wear an expression of resistance on their face and in the bold colors of their dress.[92] He is the one who kicked against the system of white supremacy altogether, though I'm not certain his revolt was a conscious one. And he is the one whose youth is immortalized in sepia-toned photographs. Daddy did not live past his thirty-fifth birthday.

Surrounded by my ancestors, I often feel like Ellison's Narra-tor, a nameless protagonist. I, too, am obsessed with understand-ing myself in the shadows of racism and oppression. With my ancestors encased in glass frames and some painted onto burlap canvas stretched over wooden crossbars, I can bear witness to their passive or audacious interpretations of their place in a bro-ken world. I can see my place in our delicate lineage. On days when I become disillusioned like Ellison's Narrator and feel the impossible weight of living in a world that is either blind to my humanity or convinced I am a threat to society because I am a Black man, I can look back at my father and grandfathers and remember that I do not have to live in the shadows.

—

The night I lost my footing after Zimmerman's acquittal in 2013, it felt as though a rug had been pulled out from under me just as I was pushing off for a sprint. At the time, I was working as a consultant, helping to shape federal public health policy initiatives through a company I founded in 2011. I was being paid to be a thought leader, someone who consumed information and presented it back as knowledge worthy of shaping public health policy. At the time, I focused on policy and advocacy for health equity. But my passion for the health of Black men was emerging.

Prior to Zimmerman's not guilty verdict, I'd asked my research associate to pull literature and a historical survey of studies on the health of Black men. Before Martin's killing, even before the police shooting deaths of Eric Garner, Michael Brown, and Freddie Gray, the Obama administration had started to take interest in the emotional and physical health of Black men. A little over a year after Zimmerman's verdict, President Obama launched My Brother's Keeper. The program's aim was to address persistent opportunity gaps facing boys and young men of color and to ensure all youth can reach their full potential.[93] I was charged with evaluating its effectiveness as a part of my work at the time. In its early form, the program was myopic. It used tired tropes of racism with good intentions, what scholar and author Ibram Kendi refers to as "uplift suasion."

—

"I grew up on this same failed strategy more than one hundred fifty years later. Generations of Black bodies have been raised by the judges of 'uplift suasion.' The judges strap the entire Black race on the Black body's back, shove the burdened Black body into White spaces, order the burdened Black body to always act in an upstanding manner. . . . I felt the burden my whole Black life to be perfect before both White people and the Black people judging whether I am representing the race well. The judges never let me just be, be myself, be my imperfect self."[94]

—IBRAM KENDI, *How to Be an Antiracist*

—

While My Brother's Keeper has since evolved to take aim at the mental health crisis in the Black male community, this evolution required seismic shifts—a pandemic and global racial justice protests of police brutality after the death of George Floyd. At its inception, My Brother's Keeper was a head nod to a trending fascination with Black men. Philosophically, the program was cliched. It pulled from a philosophy of self-responsibility, the notion that Black men have the final say in whether we successfully escape the mental, financial, educational, and occupational barriers systematically and systemically built into the fabric of American life. The discussion was intellectually dishonest and culturally stunted. It stopped short of unpacking correlations between health and system outcomes. And it did little to address the complicated task Black men face in defining what it means to be a man within a broken system that characterizes masculinity against skewed tenets of white supremacy.

Which is why after Zimmerman's acquittal, my informal studies on Black men's health became all consuming. Archaic strategies like "uplift suasion" are tried-and-failed ones. I began to see a new path forward for the healing of Black men and Black people. I wanted to create new strategies. The more I learned, the more I realized how much I did not know. I felt a personal mandate to do something with the new understanding I was developing, both of myself and of the Black male experience. No longer personal opinions that I simply expressed at dinner parties, my knowledge was beginning to feel weighty, burdensome. It was a weight that needed sharing.

—

As children, Black boys are told we are part of a club that is treated and seen differently.[95] The idea is reinforced by society but also within our own families. We are warned that we must handle our blackness and our manliness delicately, lest we pay the ultimate price: our lives. We are presented with a set of constrained gender norms and falsehoods about what it means to be a man. We adhere to the "real men don't" philosophy.[96] We don't cry. We don't love fully. Even though our experiences often leave us crying on the inside and with a desire to love and be loved without restraint. America's construct of masculinity is a manifestation of white supremacy. It was never intended for us in the first place.[97] We cannot process what it means to be a Black man without first processing what we've been told about what it means to be a man.

Yet it is impossible to fully grasp the sociological pressures Black men endure daily. This is not strictly a statement about white people or their intrinsic inability to empathize with the nonwhite experience. Black liberation has never been tied to white America's knowledge of our experience. What I'm saying is that even as a Black man, I must discern the heaviness of the load on my back, only in part, to preserve my spirit and joy. It takes tremendous energy to simply *be* while carrying the memory and vulnerability of racial traumas, while also being denied a forgiving emotional outlet.[98] But beyond our intuitive efforts of self-preservation, America has yet to lend its ear to the amassing medical and social research that qualifies the obvious impacts racism has on the health of Black men. Many have made and are making an ardent effort to scientifically baseline the experience of what it means to be Black and male in America. There is no dearth of knowledge on this matter. Rather, there is an aversion to truth.[99] The truth is all humans are pressed under one social pressure or another, often at the intersection of many. And the truth is that for Black men, society has created a particularly tight and oppressive mold. This construct traces back to slavery. Imagine living daily when everyone around you has been told—with many convinced—that you are dangerous. We are seen only how others want to see us, and their limitations of vision, in turn, place limitations on our ability to exist. Some of us, like Ralph Ellison's Narrator, conclude that we are invisible. That the world is filled with blind people who cannot or will not see our real nature. This is not a matter of throwing in the towel, but a matter of survival. Others of us survive by resisting the momentum of white power and the racist policies that attempt to anchor this power for time immemorial. Neither path is more righteous than the other. Both take an aberrant toll on the psyches and spirit of Black men.

It is quite remarkable that Black men can function in society given the current circumstances. In his book *Freedom Dreams: The Black Radical Imagination*, author and historian Robin D. G.

Kelly introduces an artful and precious coping mechanism. He suggests that Black boys and girls are born with a "third eye."[100] It is an instinctive way of looking at the world to transform what is into what can be. More than weavers of elaborate fantasies, we, the disinherited, are graced with the ability to use our imaginations to navigate a racially charged country and inequitable world. This third eye activates our dreams. Dreams of a world filled with love, joy, and freedom.

—

"'Let's make a miracle,' I shouted. 'Let's take back our pillaged eyes! Let's reclaim our sight; let's combine and spread our vision.'"

—THE NARRATOR, Ralph Ellison's *The Invisible Man*

—

I am often asked what drove me to therapy. There was no event. Rather, it was the realization that I was not myself. I remember sitting on the edge of my bed in the basement and thinking to myself, "Something isn't right." It felt like someone else was living my life, like I'd lost control of the reins. I remember being interviewed for a job. I didn't get the job. A few weeks later, the hiring manager called me and asked if I was OK. What eventually became clear to me is that depression is like bad cologne. People can smell it a mile away. Your spirits, your energy are all recognizably poor to everyone but you. For people who don't know you, you leave a bad impression. Those who do know you think that something isn't right but oftentimes are not equipped to compassionately confront you and help you on your feet. It was as if I had a dark cloud hovering over me. The faster I tried to run away from it, the more trained its target on me became.

One day, I decided to go to my primary care physician for help. I told him, "I am not feeling myself." I told him I was having trouble staying motivated for the simplest of tasks. That my patience was as thin as ice, cracking under the smallest of slights. That my sleep was erratic, as was my concentration. My doctor suggested that I "see someone." He handed me a seven-page printout with three columns of therapists' names on each sheet. My selection process consisted of closing my eyes, tracing my finger down a page, and calling the therapist whose name I'd unwittingly pointed to. When I didn't click with the first therapist, I repeated this exercise. I repeated it again and again and again. I saw white therapists and Black therapists, young and old, faith-based and agnostic, and each time[101] found myself weighed down by the exhausting task of having to convince them of the importance of my experience in the world as a Black man.[102] The act of telling my story over and over was exhausting. Each time I left a session, I felt worse than when I arrived. I kept thinking, surely this is not how I am supposed to feel. Some days, it was incredibly difficult to even get out of bed to make my way to see a therapist. One time, I was late to a therapy appointment due to D.C. subway delays. When I finally made it to the office, the therapist told me that I would need to wait until our next appointment to talk because she had a client scheduled after me and there was not enough time left. I quietly accepted her words, and then excused myself to the bathroom where I cried before making the return trip home on the subway to the safety of my basement.

When I finally connected with a therapist—Dr. Rufus Tony Spann, the man who would become the first chief clinical officer of my company Henry Health years later—it was through a friend's referral. Spann was a Black male therapist, and he could relate to my journey. Yet, finding him was just as spontaneous as my pin-the-finger routine. I learned about Spann in a conversation with a friend after asking about her marriage. I admired the connection she and her husband displayed, but she confessed to me that they previously had problems. Spann, she said, had helped them find a new path.

At first, there was nothing extraordinarily different from Spann than the others. He was warm, personable, and he listened. By our fourth session, he'd gained enough insights into my life and my depression to properly frame questions that dug beneath the surface and helped me articulate why I'd ended up sitting in the chair across from him, desperate for help. In one session, he brought a bag full of plastic building blocks. He asked me to name each major and minor responsibility I held in life, from being a father to running my own company and supporting my extended family. For each responsibility I named, Spann stacked a plastic block atop another. After about twenty blocks, he'd built a miniature wall, waist high. But without Spann's arm to brace the structure, it was incapable of standing and staying intact. At one point, the wall of blocks came crashing down. Of the blocks that fell, I had to decide which were necessary to pick up that day. In that session, I accepted the fact that I could not be who I had been. The vision of who I thought I had to be—my idealized self—was unsustainable. I would have to reimagine how I managed my responsibilities. I would have to reimagine life.

I often wondered what Spann wrote in his notebook after exercises like this, but I didn't care. The conversation was one I desperately needed. Finally, somebody was able to help me begin to understand myself. Finally, I was in a safe space, able to be honest about my experiences and the world I was living in. Finally, I could speak my truth, be believed, and be heard. That was life changing.

Eventually, I had to change therapists because Spann did not accept my insurance, and my financial well was running dry. Spann referred me to Dr. Darius Driskell. It was Driskell who told me in 2016 that every conscious Black man needs to be in therapy. Perhaps he was being rhetorical when he said this. I took him literally. His words affirmed the deep impact of the racialized experiences I'd shared with him about my daily life. I may have been working through my own challenges, but that session was an anchor for my understanding of what it would take to help Black men heal from their traumas.

—

It is late in the day, but I still have hours to go before I will be home, at rest. Still, I feel energized, though slightly apprehensive. I sit in my car and sip a cup of coffee. It is my fourth cup that day. It is 2017, and I've just arrived at East Friendship Baptist Church in D.C. I am not here for a service. I am here to lead a focus group of Black men who have expressed interest in receiving mental health therapy. For the past year, I've been studying the works of Dr. Sherman James, Harold Neighbors, Dr. Norma Day-Vines, among others—the leading clinical researchers behind the empirical body of work that establishes correlations between mental and physical health and racism. With their help, and a team of therapists, we are designing a model of therapy that honors race and culture, particularly the experience of Black men. We are hosting focus groups to determine whether there is an interest among Black men in receiving therapy designed with them in mind. I take a final sip of coffee, then make my way to the church's back entrance and into the fellowship hall. Twenty or so metal folding chairs have been arranged in a circle. I take my seat just as the hall's front door entrance opens. A flood of men pours into the room, and I can feel my pulse rising. I question whether the fourth cup of coffee was necessary. I stand to welcome the men, make a point to shake each of their hands, look them in the eye, and thank them for showing up. They take their seats, and the nervous chatter dies down. In the silence, I can hear their breath, my breath. I invite them to listen to it too, to hold their inhales and extend their exhales. After a few deep breaths, I ask them to close their eyes, to quiet their thoughts. We hold this space for a few seconds, and then one of the men begins to weep. I invite us to open our eyes, and I see the man who is crying. He is holding his head, and the man next to him has a hand placed on his shoulder. "I can't remember the last time I allowed myself to be still like this, to be quiet like this with others around," the crying man says. He continues, "I'm tired, but I didn't realize just how tired I was." Another man lifts a handkerchief from his pocket and begins to dab his eyes. Still, another man's eyes tear up, and he lets them fall down his cheeks. A knot forms in my throat, and I am speechless. Sometimes, there is nothing to say when you realize you are precisely where you are meant to be. The silence is enough.

—

2018 JOURNAL ENTRY

"What do I know for sure? I don't have a back-up plan.
Because I don't have a passion for anything else."

—

It is a year after the launch of the first focus groups. It is a chilly afternoon in October, and I have yet to warm up with a cup of coffee. It is unusual for me to put off my morning coffee ritual, but once again, the days are moving fast. New things are important to me. I scrub a sticky table in the common area of D.C.'s 1776, a brick-and-mortar hub for incubators and start-ups just blocks from the White House. I am in good spirits, though presently annoyed with the dirty furniture. A journalist sits at the table, waiting to start an interview about my newly launched digital mental health company for Black men, Henry Health.

"The first thing you should know is that my story is about striving to create a better life for myself and other Black men," I tell the reporter. She fumbles for her phone, pulls up a voice memo app, and presses a bright red button.

"Mind if I record?" she asks.

"Not at all." I laugh. "I've been telling this story for years now."

It is true. Five years earlier, after Zimmerman's acquittal, I posed a question to a close circle of peers: Could being a Black man in this world make you sick?[103] I sought out philanthropists to help turn my informal probe into a national survey called "What's Killing Black Men?" It was an inquiry of the self. And it was an inquiry into the racial power construct that defined the systems and policies of America that were, I suspected, making me and other Black men sick.

"The second thing you should know is that my story of striving to create a better life as a Black man in America is not unique."

I explain that as a part of my multi-year inquiry, I'd met with countless Black men who shared similar journeys to mine. Their stories became the backbone of my new life purpose: increase the well-being and lifespan of Black men in America.

"The one thing we all shared was a thirst for a better life while realizing that the deck was stacked against us. And when you know that the deck is stacked against you, you try harder. You exert more effort for simple tasks.[104] I did that. I tried to do everything right, but that type of pressure is unsustainable. It is scientifically unhealthy. I tried to adjust in my life to manage the stress, but I couldn't make them fast enough. Soon, I found myself in the throes of a debilitating depression."

I have learned how to tell my story. Through its telling, I have practiced again and again the release of shame and the need to hide it. This is my truth: I became the subject of my own research and found my way out of a debilitating depression by building a mental health care model that could serve Black men like me, and one day soon other disinherited people. And I have learned that it is important to share it.

—

2019 JOURNAL ENTRY

"The last few years have been unhappy years. I have found little joy in my life. It has impacted every part of me. But what I have experienced is part of life. I, too, must experience hardship. It has brought me patience, maturity, and contentment. I'd like to believe that I've lost a lot of my ego. I now know that I don't have all the answers and my best plans sometimes don't work. So, I invite the spirit of God to work through me."

—

It's late in the afternoon on a fall day in 2020, a year that feels like a long-extended gesture of "too little too late." I am speaking with Dr. Sherman James over a video call, my eighth call that day. James is a Black epidemiologist and health researcher most known for his concept "John Henryism," which attributes the premature deaths of Black people to prolonged exposure to the stresses of discrimination and racism. We are talking about the tipping point in his career. After forty years of research into the social determinants of racial and ethnic health disparities, and in particular the impact on Black men, his work is finally getting the exposure it deserves. James's pinnacle has been a long time coming and now that it is here, it is bittersweet. All it took was George Floyd and a world paused in a state of reflection as the result of a devastating pandemic.

James, too, started his journey to help improve the world around him as a fresh-faced college student. In 1971, he began his research into the correlations between ethnicity and health. Two years later, James received his PhD in psychology from Washington University in St. Louis. By the mid-'80s, the focus of his work had narrowed as an emerging social epidemiologist.

From 1983 to the mid-'90s, he suggested, through no less than forty-five published journal articles, that an entire segment of research was needed to assess socioeconomic influences on the health of Black people and Black men specifically. His research under the banner of Duke University's Sanford School of Public Policy drew correlations between hypertension in Black men and psychosocial factors unique to their experience in a racialized world. James theorized that "repetitive high-effort coping with difficult social and economic stressors is a major contributor to racial and socioeconomic disparities in hypertension and related cardiovascular diseases."[105] In other words, when someone works hard in a system that has not afforded them an equal opportunity to succeed, their health suffers.[106]

James's career is cresting during an unprecedented racial reckoning, with media, corporate America, and policy shapers citing his years-long research. Yet, he is set to retire in a few months. On this call, I am hoping to unearth some new insight for these racialized times before he makes his leave.

"In my early work, there was little to no resistance, even though I fully expected there to be," James says. It goes without saying, but James expected resistance because his research poked holes in the white power construct. It suggested—loosely at first, then later more poignantly—that white supremacy was bad for nonwhite people's health.

"The lack of resistance was not an outcome of altruism in the medical research world. It was because I didn't explicitly say that racism was a determining factor in the health of marginalized populations," James says. "Back then, terms like 'structural racism' were not as ubiquitous as they are now."

Instead, James shaped his research under titles like *Socioeconomic*

Influences on Coronary Heart Disease in Black Populations and *Psychosocial and Environmental Factors in Black Hypertension*. Accurate titles, even if they had to skirt an otherwise direct statement of racism's impact on well-being to make it past the editor's desk.

"There was a fifteen-year period when no one wanted to explicitly say that racism was the problem." James is smiling as he says this. I can't help but wonder if it's because he can finally say these things out loud without having to justify his experience. "But in the mid-'90s, I started to connect the dots."

It would take more than thirty years for James's research to land on fertile ground.

"The irony is not lost on me, Kevin," James says, still smiling. "I am wrapping up my empirical research, preparing to retire, and the world is finally ready to listen to what I've been saying. The question is, do I retire now and recoup some of the years that the stress of this work has almost certainly taken from me? Or do I press on, knowing what I know about stress and its impact on the life expectancy of Black men in America?"

James's smile widens, and he laughs. He knows, as do I, the answer to the question.

—

2019 JOURNAL ENTRY

"I see that God is calling me to a higher place of service. I still find myself discouraged from time to time, but I see little reminders along the way to help me remember the darkness I left to come into the light. While the last few years of my life have been filled with disappointment and much unhappiness, I am grateful for the light that grows brighter inside of me, day by day."

The Joy of the Disinherited

"This joy that I have, the world didn't give it to me. . . .
The world can't take it away."

—"THIS JOY," by Shirley Caesar

The water-laid soil surrounding Ella Mae's home in Tucker, Arkansas, has history. Most dirt does. My grandmother's dirt hails from ancient floodplains of river systems. It is made up of old deposits of marine sediments that took hundreds of thousands of years to develop, the soil horizon primed just in time for our ancestors to cultivate after arriving on America's shores in the underbelly of slave ships. Which is to say it is fertile soil. Good for producing cotton, soybeans, feed grain, and corn. And roses. In front of her home, Ella Mae planted a single rose bush.

Ella Mae was born twenty-three miles up the road from where her roses grew, in a community called Keo. She was born into a large family. Her family tree—my family tree—resembles a magnolia, the kind with multiple trunks to support a sprawling web of limbs. At the base, before vertical shoots grow long and distant from their roots, there is my great-grandfather John

Quincy Shivers. Ella Mae often tells me the story of Grandpa Shivers, who was born into slavery in 1848. When he was freed, he took to the land as a farmer. By the time he died, Grandpa Shivers had become a successful owner and tiller of that rich Delta farmland. But many of his children, drawn to the promises of the North, migrated to Chicago, leaving the family farm for city life. When Grandpa Shivers died, with no one to care for the crops, his land was sold. The profits of the sale were divided among his children and his children's children. Ella Mae was a teenager when she received her inheritance, a "decent-sized check, back then," she says.

Every Christmas, my grandmother tells the story of her inheritance. The story does not begin with Grandpa Shivers's death. Rather, it is told in succession to the story of her mother's death. Ella Mae lost her mother on a Christmas Day at the age of seven. "First my mama. A few years later, Grandpa Shivers." Ella Mae found a place to live and work in the home of the Albrights, a white family that later hired her husband, George, as foreman on their farm. Each year at Christmastime, she holds space for her dear mother, gone too soon. In her telling of the story, she is keenly aware of the breadth of her loss preceding the inheritance. The loss of her father, of her mother, but also a homestead on which her family could build a foundation, a future. How her inheritance stemmed, like one of those leggy offshoots on her family tree, from the sacrifices of those who tilled the earth before her. She understands how easily the inheritance of the disinherited can fall limp, deadened in a cold winter if not nurtured and pruned.

—

Know this, Kevin: When a person finds their purpose, it changes everything.

A preacher is speaking a good word into my heart. It is 2017 and an unusual situation: me in a pastor's office, seeking some divine guidance, his message falling on fertile ground. I am surprised by the pastor's intuitive read on my waning spirit. Contrary to the setting, I am not meeting him for prophecies of the soul. Rather, at my accountant's suggestion, I am meeting Max to help me hack my way out of financial disrepair. Several years into a debilitating depression, I'd lost my footing. I'd concluded that the debt and financial responsibility I'd found myself in was nearly impossible to overcome. Worse, I couldn't parse the chicken from the egg. I was unsure if I became depressed and then lost my financial bearings or vice versa. And did the order even matter? When I suggested to my accountant, Chris Thinker, that I file for bankruptcy, he eschewed the idea.

"That will follow you for years," Chris said. "Call Pastor Melvin Maxwell over at D.C.'s East Friendship Baptist Church instead."

"Chris, I'm not calling no preacher," I said.

"Trust me. Max is different," he said. "He's a businessman who happens to be a man after God's own heart."

I had Max's number for weeks before calling him. When I finally did, our phone call lasted three hours. We discussed my financial situation, but we also discussed matters of the soul. Namely, my soul. Max championed my spiritual welfare on that call in a way that brought me to my knees, and then to my feet. That was two days ago. Now, I am sitting directly across from him believing for the first time in years that God and the world has not forsaken me. That I am precisely where I need to be.

Still, I find myself waiting for our conversation to turn to a ploy to add me to the church's headcount on Sundays. My faith is one with complications, occasionally in need of a stent to widen areas of my heart that constricted at one time or another to protect it from the sharp aim of the church's judgement. Even with this man of God, my guard is up. I fix my eyes on the floor, fold my arms across my chest and sink back into the chair. I am coming to terms with my spiritual reality and am quietly kicking and screaming en route: I am not in a place to negotiate my preferred sources of divine guidance. I need something more than the prescribed way of "manning up." My well of self-sufficiency has run dry. At this moment, I need someone to look beyond my legacy of successfully bootstrapping life because at this moment, I've run out of straps. I need my waning spirit to be seen simply for the sake of being fully seen.

"You are so convinced that God has abandoned you, Kevin," Max says. "But God is in the darkness with you."[107]

—

All of us need something to believe in.[108] Even the atheist has confidence that a well-built chair will hold their weight. Even Black matriarchs who have buried sons, brothers, daughters, and husbands into an earth saturated with the blood and sweat of ancestors will sing about "this joy" that they have. I can still hear some of their voices, echoing against ceiling rafters of a country church on Sunday, rising above the choir's refrain, and the rattle of steel oscillating wall fans. Anyone within earshot heard about "this joy"—its good measure, how it'd been pressed down and shaken together. These matriarchs were clear about their joy's origins: The world did not give it to them. The world could not take it away.

While setting a pot of beans to boil or pinning up a bedsheet to dry in the sun, Ella Mae would softly hum about how she was "coming up on the right side of the mountain," not the rough side. That she was "holding God's powerful hand" and "doing her best to make it in." My mother modeled Ella Mae's determined optimism and stubborn love in her refusal of a mediocre life and in her prayers laden with gratitude and thanksgiving. These days, I often think about my mother's buoyant hope and Ella Mae's songs, about her rose bushes. I think about these private joys they and my ancestors held onto through long days and lonely nights. I think about the remarkability of their capacity to find the heart to sing. And above all, I think about how this joy might be replicated for other heavy souls to soar.

—

In Max's office, I am telling him about my all-consuming inquiry into this question: What's killing Black men? I tell him about John Henryism and the body of research that validates racism's deadly impact on the mental and physical health of Blacks and other disinherited people.[109] I share with him my vision to create a digital platform that gives people who look and feel like me access to therapists who understand people who look and feel like we do.

"You are advancing into a dark space while in a dark space yourself," Max says. "Trauma is a safe space for the enemy to work."

As I lean in toward Max, rather than remain recoiled in the

slouch I began our meeting with, I am starting to believe this session is the beginning of something good. He sees my depression. He sees the effects of my spiraling and sprawling inquiry into my oppressed mind. He believes me when I say I want to find a way out, once and for all, and that I want to light the path of my journey so that others may follow. In a matter of months, I will meet with Oliver Simms III, a University of Arkansas at Fayetteville alumnus and global tech sales leader in a division of Broadcom. Simms will ask if I've considered a career in digital health, prompting me to launch Henry Health with him as a co-founder and COO. Henry Health will be the first iteration of my mental wellness company for Black men, named after the legend of John Henry and Dr. Sherman James's theory of John Henryism. Max will take the helm of my contracting company so I can focus on my vision for a new mental health care system that does not ignore race and culture. Investors will commit their money, talents, and time to the vision—angels, accelerators, advocates. Henry Health will evolve to meet the therapy needs of the broader Black community and then other underserved populations in the mental health care system. In 2020, I will rename the company Hurdle, a nod to invisible mental health care barriers. Then, a global pandemic will paralyze the world. People everywhere will experience life-altering change, heartbreaking loss, isolation, and the white noise of their own thoughts. But depression and anxiety will rise sharpest in America's Black communities.[110] Young Black men will die at higher rates from the pandemic's devastating virus. George Floyd, Black, handcuffed, and unable to move, will be murdered at the knee of a white Minneapolis policeman. Hundreds of the largest corporations in America will give their employees a paid holiday for Juneteenth, which commemorates the emancipation of Blacks. Hurdle will raise a $5 million capital investment by the year's end to expand its culturally competent mental health care services. By the following summer, Juneteenth, named for June 19, 1865, the day when Blacks in Texas were the last in the country told of their freedom two years after it was granted, will be designated a federal holiday.

But today, sitting across from Max on a winter day in 2017, I am a victim of unresolved repeat racial and generational trauma. Today, Max says, I am advancing into enemy territory with a mark on my back.

"You will get challenged across all dimensions of your existence," Max tells me. "You will need God."[111]

—

My faith in a higher power, in God has taken many forms— religious, spiritual, skeptical, utilitarian, constant. I have wrestled in the dark with deified representations of half-truths and emerged bruised, limping. There is great consequence for the disinherited when we blindly believe in dogmas that sprout unquestioning compliance. Left unchecked, these misbeliefs will keep us down. Our misbeliefs will keep us right where a racialized society would have us convinced we should be, when really, God would have us dancing like David.

In my efforts to reclaim joy, I tried different paths—the spiritual, the intellectual. I misstepped often, sometimes with sass. I became lost in the misbeliefs I once looked to for guidance. The belief that the only real love is sacrificial. That I could outrun America's racial past and my past by trying harder, always harder. That liberation for the disinherited is tied to an awakening of the oppressor. That joy was a privileged state of being. In that delicate surgery of the psyche to rid myself of the cumbersome, albeit holy, shame of the oppressed, I lost things. I lost relationships, my marriage, for one. Olivia did her best and protected our children during my dark period, but eventually, it was too just too much for her to stay. Our divorce was amicable, and we strategized a separation that would not hinder our children's sense of security, belonging, and love. But I still grieve for the loss of the future we once had together. In the process of examining my life and beliefs, I also lost trite ways of hoping, loving, and believing. I lost old visions, old passions. I tried to pray my way to joy. When things got hard, I prayed harder. Convinced that God had abandoned me, I believed that if I could simply pinpoint the reason why I was left to wander a desert of darkness then I could re-engineer a path back to God's favor.[112] If I could reconnect with God, then God would rescue me from my trouble. When I didn't receive immediate guidance, I became convinced of this misbelief: I had somehow disgraced myself and God. I drifted in and out of pleas for God to show me what I had done wrong.

When that didn't work, I took up the purely intellectual path. I studied the "dark night of the soul," a concept Eckhart Tolle articulated that describes eruptions in our lives that can lead to deep feelings of meaninglessness, but also to deep awakenings. I read theological books and clinical studies. I needed to understand what was happening to me. It was too much to bear by myself. Yet the deeper I dug, the more I felt distant from God.

—

"A hand touched me and set me trembling on my hands and knees. He said, 'Daniel, you who are highly esteemed, consider carefully the words I am about to speak to you, and stand up, for I have now been sent to you.' And when he said this to me, I stood up trembling."

—DANIEL 10:10-11

—

Of all the broken characters in the Bible, I identify most with Daniel. The Old Testament book of Daniel is considered an apocalypse, a literary genre in which a heavenly reality is revealed to a human recipient. In this case, Daniel is that recipient. He waits twenty-one days to receive God's help. God delivers, but not before Daniel breaks down, questioning everything he's ever known about himself and God's divine promise for his life. I can imagine Daniel in those weeks. Piqued, withdrawn, his impatience spilling over into an anger that manifests itself in expletives directed at the small missteps of the day—a stubbed toe, a burned meal. Perhaps a loss of interest in the things that used to excite him. The feeling of abandonment in the deafening silence where God's voice should have been. And amid all the despondency, an obstinate hope for himself and his people. On the good days, I imagine his hope for the salvation of his people got him through the day. On other days, I imagine his hope felt more like a curse than a vision.

My struggle, too, has at times seemed daunting. Once my vision to add ten years onto the life expectancy of Black men in America was articulated, I moved into enemy territory. I have felt powerful forces push against me, both in the waking world and in the spiritual realm. These forces trying to derail my plans to help the disinherited discover and reclaim joy take the form of racist policies and systems. But they also manifest as spiritual and mental burdens. Exposed to repeat trauma and oppression, we the disinherited run the risk of believing that God has abandoned us. That is what happened to me. Prior to experiencing depression, there had never been a time when I called on God and didn't get the help I needed. Like Daniel, when I couldn't hear that inner voice assuring me of my inherent divinity, I became convinced that I was alone, left to languish on the vine.

—

Ella Mae never had many material possessions. The most elaborate piece of furniture she ever owned was a sectional couch that sat in the parlor room of her small home. The same home that her husband, George, built with money he saved from working for the Albrights. The couch was a gift from her son, Johnny, who knew how important it was for Ella Mae to have a space where she could "take a look" at all her grandbabies. The same Johnny that was swept away by an undertow in the Arkansas River at the age of twenty-seven. Ella Mae didn't have much, but she was resourceful in the needed materials to care for the roses that adorned her doorstep in Tucker, Arkansas. She rarely had time to herself. Ella Mae tended to Ada Albright, the matriarch of the Albright home, and the Albright children. She tended to her own children and grandchildren. And she tended to her roses. She nurtured them all year long, mixing garden compost into the soil to keep them fertilized and peat moss to help the plant hold the soil's nutrients. When needed, she cut back dead and damaged canes to half the previous year's growth until she found the healthy white centers. In the winter, she mounded the base of the bush with cedar mulch to protect it in its dormant state. By early spring, the red blooms were plenty. Plenty enough so that in May, she could clip a dozen flowers to decorate her dinner table on Mother's Day and still have a dozen blooms left on the bush to keep her doorstep decorated.

Recently, I planted my own rose bushes. I am building a flower garden. There is also lavender, hibiscus, and begonias. I think often of Ella Mae and her single rose bush, of her perennial bouquet. This year, I, too, will make a bouquet when my flowers are in full bloom and in need of pruning. Some days, I daydream about the arrangement—an assortment of red roses with a few stalks of purple lavender, taking care to trim any brown or dead leaves, finding the perfect vase to complement the bend in the flowers' stems and the architecture of their petals. The small things bring me joy.

—

"Again and again, he came back to the inner life of the individual. With increasing insight and startling accuracy, he placed his finger on the 'inward center' as the crucial arena where the issues would determine the destiny of his people."

—REV. HOWARD THURMAN, *Jesus and the Disinherited*[113]

—

These days, I doubt freely, while holding tight to God's love. I believe with a healthy dose of suspicion. I allow old beliefs, beliefs that were shaped by systems, not spirit, to unravel. I weave together new ones. On a rare Sunday, I sit in a pew at the back of a church, slipping in and out quietly, confining my fellowship to the greeters at the church doors. Other Sundays, when the air is warm and the sun is out, I sip cold wine, trim dead leaves from my rose bushes and daydream about my future, my kids' futures, and the future of this country we call home. I reflect on how our human story is epic, tragic, and miraculous. How when we fall, we fall hard, but in our moments of altruistic compassion, we soar.

One of those Sunday mornings, while tending to my flower garden, I was reminded of a time when I felt like I could soar as high as I could dream. It was that first inkling of ambition that swelled in my chest and made me want to be somebody. The February after the Christmas my daddy died, I recited Dr. Martin Luther King Jr.'s "I Have a Dream Speech" before Little Rock's entire Gibbs Elementary School. The school had around 300 students, not counting the parents and community members in attendance that day. I was ten. My teacher, Mrs. Berdine Ready, encouraged me to deliver the speech as a part of our school's Black History Month assembly. She was the same teacher who'd read my father's obituary in the newspaper over the holidays and created a safe space for me to grieve, allowing my pain and sadness to coexist with the normal rhythms of the school day. At the time, it seemed fitting that I should recite Dr. King's speech. My mother's sister, Autra Lee, gave me a record of his speeches a year prior, and I'd taken it upon myself to memorize his most famous one. As an adult with children of my own, I now understand Ms. Ready's intentions in selecting me. Sure, I knew the words. More importantly, Ms. Ready knew I *needed* to be on that stage. Still raw from losing my daddy, I needed King's words on my lips, and I needed to speak his words to this crowd. Gibbs was a stone's throw away from my family's home in Village Square. This was my community. This was my great cloud of witnesses. King's dream was my dream, was our dream. If any dignity—my own, my siblings', my mother's, my father's—had been lost in Daddy's death, it was restored through the communal recitation and receiving of King's words. In church, we call this a pulling down of the spirit. A collective call on the heavens to invade our earthly space so that we might heal and dance again. In therapy, this is called an intervention. Call it what you will—the spirit, a sixth sense, an intervention—that day I was given a gift that no one could take away from me, a knowledge of the disinherited that is passed on to one another in our time of need. That something that tells you somewhere someone loves you no matter how you are treated in this world.

—

As a little boy, I learned early on that spirituality flows through the Black community like the blood in our veins. It is life giving. And like blood, the communal spirit instinctively rushes to the site of our wounds to begin the immediate work of healing. In this way, we cannot talk about healing the mental wounds of Black people without talking about Black spirituality. We have long held on to a complex faith that has informed our ability to believe—against all odds—that we are more than what we have been told we are. That we are connected to the Divine. This is what our ancestors clinged to so tightly, this is what they passed on in song and story. And this faith has been our staying power. I learned it through the hymns Ella Mae sang, and I saw it in my mother's hopeful eyes. But this belief alone cannot piece us back together when we break into a million pieces. Sometimes, we must let go of what we were and instead use the broken pieces of what's left to create a beautiful mosaic. Conventional wisdom holds that trauma scars us for life. We are often led to believe trauma wreaks psychological havoc—and only havoc—that affects everything from our sleep cycles to our relationships to our very will to live. I felt this during the darkest points of my depression, and for a long time, I believed my trauma had no positive offerings. Then, I discovered the work of pioneering psychologist Stephen Joseph. Joseph counters the conventional wisdom about trauma in his book *What Doesn't Kill Us.* He picks apart the popular conception of trauma and lifts a startling, though obvious, revelatory fact: Many people emerge from traumatic experiences stronger, wiser, and more fulfilled, despite having endured great emotional pain.[114] At one point, his concept inspired me to put one foot in front of the other and, more importantly, intentionally recognize the small and necessary evolutions I was making from despair to hope. However, we must take Joseph's concept a step further. He builds from the notion that trauma is either a singular or finite event in a person's lifetime. But what of the Black American experience? The disinherited life? A life that is arguably one long traumatic event, from cradle to grave?

It has been long held that Black people were not particularly interested in mental health services—be it stigma, affordability, our religious beliefs, or assumptions from the designers of our existing mental health care system asserting we did not have the emotional or intellectual capacity for therapy.[115]

The truth is the current mental health system was never designed for Black people.[116] Historically, the field of psychology has labeled Black people as simple, unable to process emotions. These are just layers of the same great lie about intellectual inferiority across races. In truth, oppression robs you of your identity. Our world has long told Black people that we are less than, then required us to be the hero of our own stories.

But for those without the resources and support network to rebuild, what of them? For those who have not had access to culturally relevant health and wellness resources the way I have, what of them? Between the lines of Thurman's theological apologetics, he often offers shortcuts to spiritual well-being for the disinherited. They are easily missed, nestled between his prophetic musings. Shortcuts like practicing mindfulness when ironing your clothes. Or taking pride in how you dress even if there are only two shirts hanging in your closet. The disinherited have had to lean on these small yet profound habits of wellness for millennia. Learning to sing and laugh under the hot sun of oppression has been our salvation. Still, it is a poetic form of bootstrapping, pulling our happiness up by thin straps of daily healthy habits when, really, entire systems need revolutionizing. Until the trauma of the disinherited experience is accepted as a grave reality, our systems—from education, to financial, to health care—will stop short of rectifying the inequities that keep us with our backs pressed against the wall.

—

The day I meet with Max, I inch away from my emotional wall. Preparing to leave, I stand, though I do not move. I remain in the doorway and realize I need to tell him one more thing: "Days after Christmas, when I was ten years old, my father died of a cocaine-induced brain aneurysm." I immediately feel a lifting of my spirit. "I needed you to know that about me, about my father," I say. Max nods his head slowly. "Don't stop telling your father's story," he says. "His story is your story. And it is the story of so many others."

—

I used to divide the world into darkness and light, insisting on duality rather than accepting the beauty in both. Now I see the darkness for what it was: a conduit of light. In her book *Learning to Walk in the Dark*, author Barbara Brown Taylor writes, "It is always night somewhere, giving people the darkness they need to see, feel, and think things that hide out during the day."[117]

For decades, my darkness was pervasive, settling in my pain in plain sight, in the light of day. The pain of my father's perpetual absence, the pain of being judged for my melanin rather than the contents of my heart. I hid all this pain in my relentless striving for what was prescribed as the good life. Eventually, the sun set on my journey. In the twilight, I pressed on until I could no longer walk. Darkness set in, and without a light to guide the path, I was forced to be still. I learned to place a finger on the inward center of my being and acknowledge the spiritual war that was raging in and around me. I began to address the issues, one by one, that were determining the destiny of my joy. In the darkness, I accepted the ubiquity of my experience as a member of America's disinherited. In the darkness, I made this vow: I would help create a safe space for all when I made it back to the light.

MY DUNGEON SHOOK, AND THE CHAINS ARE OFF:

An Open Letter to Anna, Ella, and Davis

"My Dungeon Shook," an essay by James Baldwin, was first published in 1962 in *The Progressive*. Written as a letter to Baldwin's nephew, the essay was intended to commemorate the 100th anniversary of the Emancipation Proclamation. With deep respect for Baldwin and his literary genius, I offer a 2021 version of the letter.

Dear Anna, Ella, and Davis,

I am writing this letter for fear that I may not be able to speak these words to you.

Lately, your Uncle Billy and I have been talking a lot about death. In 2020, not only did we lose Grandma Sue, but Billy also lost three of his friends to deaths related to the COVID-19 virus. Even before the pandemic hallowed out a generation of Black men, a year ago we laid to rest Mr. Brownlee, my mentor, and Uncle John, my Daddy's youngest brother—two Black men gone too soon.

From the time you learned to talk and pray your own prayers, you were taught the role that loss plays in life. This ancient truth is your patrimony: Death and loss are at the core of all existence, a prelude to life. Still, no matter its inevitability, the life-death-life cycle contains a tragic power that can ultimately bring the best of us to our knees. I have been waiting to find the time, the courage, the strength to stand up, brush my knees off, and tell you other truths. There may never be a perfect moment, and although I have done my level best to expand my vocabulary, I am not sure that my voice will hold long enough to adequately express how I feel about these matters. I write these things so you might know and live wholly.

One day, I woke up, and I found myself living in the basement of our home. It didn't happen overnight. Like most transformations in life, it happened slowly, as Hemingway says, then suddenly. I made my bed in the basement because your mother and I needed space. I have warned you: Marriage is complicated. Two people can love each other very much and still not see eye to eye. Life is full of contradictions, and the love your mother and I share is just one example of this. One thing I think that she'd agree with is that I have given every fiber inside of me to create a fulfilling life for you and instill in you a hope that I didn't have growing up. When my father died, I'd already been struck by the angel of death, having lost my uncle—my mother's brother—and my grandfather. At a young age, I lost my willingness to become too devoted to someone.[118] I realized we will one day lose the people we love, sometimes unexpectedly. I wish I could shield you from this reality, but already you have lost two uncles and a grandmother.

When my daddy died, I was only ten years old. I know you get tired of hearing about the loss of my father. I repeat it often because I think you are lucky to have a father. I am not puffed up with pride when I say this; I wear my fatherly flaws on my sleeve. I say this because I know what it's like to grow up without a father's approval and love. Up until three years ago, I was angry with my daddy. I was angry with him for leaving me in a world that snubs its nose at fatherless Black children, and then shuns those kids when they grow up to be fatherless Black men. It took me experiencing the valley of darkness to see his life differently. Now, I see his dignity through his troubles.

You should know that your grandfather had a mean daddy. Absolutely no one has anything good to say about him. I know this because years ago I sought out the true story of our paternal lineage. One spring day, I found it in a man named Wolf, your great-grandfather's brother. He insisted I call him Wolf. I asked Wolf a simple question: "What was my grandfather like?" Wolf responded, "Your grandfather wasn't worth a shit." He said it with such resolution that I knew Wolf had told me all I needed to know. That the way my father lived and the choices he made weren't done in a vacuum of grim self-interest, even if it felt that way when I was a child. I know now that my father lived his life in resistance to his broken home, a broken world. He never had any illusions of assimilating to it, so long as the traumas of his childhood haunted him. No one dare shares all the details of buried trauma, but the consensus is that your great-grandfather inflicted the kind of damage that impacts generations.[119] My father never had the chance to overcome his childhood trauma. But if he did, I am sure he would stand before me as I am writing to you now to say, "I am sorry."

You now know that I suffered from depression. These days, I imagine my mental health feels like a talking point. But we know all too well how real and how painful my depression was—not just for me, but for you and your mother. It's been said that you should only apologize for the things you don't intend to repeat. Here, then, is where I say I am sorry. Here is where I admit my depression impacted our family. It changed the course of our family's life. I am sorry for the times I was short with you. I am sorry for the times when I read you your rights for no particular reason.[120]

Davis, I especially owe you an apology. As my only son and the eldest, you carried the brunt of my arrows. I put more on your shoulders. I naively thought that you should be able to handle more. And in believing this, I unconsciously placed my own pain, my father's pain, and his father's pain on your back. I am telling you again that I am sorry because I need you to know that this yoke is not yours to bear alone.

We cannot break the cycle of life and death, but we can address the generational trauma that robs us of our potential. We did not create this trauma, but it is ours. It is a relic of centuries past, a time when my grandfather's father's father was enslaved to his white owners in southwest Arkansas. This inherited burden of enslavement requires that we help each other remove the chains.[121] First, from our own wrists. Then, from one another, and finally, from our minds. My chains are off now, and I need to do everything I can to free you.

The world will give you enough to take to the therapist's office—an intrinsic fear of the police, the polite sting of racial microaggressions in the grocery store and around the watercooler.[122] If there are any chains from my depression arresting you, I will help you take them off.

The good news for you is that you are growing up in an age of racial reckoning. America, and the world at large, is waking up to the pain that our family, and other families like us, have shouldered disproportionately for far too long. George Floyd's murder at the knee of a Minnesota police officer accelerated this recognition.[123] But it didn't start with Floyd, or Ahmaud Arbery, or Breonna Taylor, may they rest in power. Eight years ago, some well-meaning people ignited this reckoning after Trayvon Martin, then again after Michael Brown, and again after Freddie Gray. Sixty-five years earlier in a bygone era of America's racial history, a young, twenty-six-year-old minister, Dr. Martin Luther King Jr., delivered the sermon "Pride Versus Humility: The Parable of the Pharisee and the Publican" at Dexter Avenue Baptist Church in Atlanta. It was a sermon that would set off a movement for civil rights following the murder of a young Black boy named Emmett Till at the hands of two white men.

What I'm saying is that this reckoning has been a long time coming, and I am sure you feel it in your bones, but do you feel it in your minds? All change begins in the mind, which is why I constantly plead with you to watch your thoughts. Especially now. Now, as many of our white brothers and sisters wake up to the reality of our rightful place among the stars. Now, more than ever, you must prepare your minds.

James Baldwin wrote, "If the word integration means anything, this is what it means: that we, with love, shall force our brothers [and sisters] to see themselves as they are, to cease fleeing from reality and begin to change it."[124] Our family, and dare I say every Black family in America, knows intrinsically that racism impacts every aspect of life. It is the same knowing that drew me to Wolf in search of a truth that was buried deep in my marrow. It is a tacit knowledge that is being made explicit in the videos of anti-Black police brutality that go viral, the videos you know I vowed to never watch again after Martin's murder shook me to my core. What I'm saying is that this knowledge of white supremacy's pervasive and gross pull on life in America is slowly becoming ubiquitous. The inequity of our country is no longer a quiet-kept secret. It is a knowledge of the masses.

But the pervasiveness of an idea does not intuit action. As Ibram X. Kendi wrote in 2019, "To be an anti-racist is a radical choice in the face of this [our] history, requiring radical reorientation of our consciousness."[125] After Martin, I committed to doing my part to reorient my conscience and to help change the reality of the disinherited through my work in mental health. I began my work naive to the great forces of racism and stereotyping that I was up against. The deeper and deeper I went in my work, the more I understood my opposition and my oppressors—our healing, the reclaiming of the joy of the disinherited, is the antithesis of their ill-designed systems. But these oppressive systems are built on the bedrock of an ancient lie: that our healing is synonymous to their demise.[126]

Many of our white brothers and sisters are confronting this lie. More importantly, they are seeking truth. They are looking inward and wondering when, if, and how they have been a part of the oppression of Black people and the disinherited. With the same surgical precision that we have had to apply to our own damaged psyches, they are uncovering the root of this lie. And that lie is this: scarcity, the false idea that there isn't enough for everyone and so some must take up an inferior position on the earth. You know this goes against our family's theology. When God created the heavens and earth, He created all that we needed to thrive. Scarcity is human made. Yet in America, the powerful have always used the idea of scarcity as a tool to pit people against one another—white people against Black people, men against women, Christians against Muslims, and on it goes. You can hear this message of scarcity in the argument that we should close America's borders because Brown people are taking away jobs. The bully influencer behind the drapes of hatred is scarcity. I am not convinced that hatred is a natural human trait. It is taught, but its foundation is strong enough to last for generations. The challenge we have in America is that the systems we rely on—housing, education, physical and mental health care—have been built on the lie of scarcity. When this belief makes its way into our systems, the outcome is disastrous. We vie and scrape for "me and my home," with little to no thought for how our neighbors will get by. We have seen how the lie of scarcity destroys hundreds of thousands of lives, and we are seeing an urgent, outright rejection of it. As the pandemic hushed the din of our busy lives in 2020, the earth turned slower and we—all of us—were forced to see each other at a deeper level.

I can't say with certainty that things will change in your lifetime. What I know for sure is that change is the only constant. Humanity will continue to evolve. I pray that humanity's evolution will reveal its truer self. But we can't stop at prayer. There is work for you, too. You must guard your thoughts and protect your self-image. Remember, change starts in the mind. Heal the mind, and we can heal the relationship between human beings. We can mark the supreme moment when human dignity is divinely held. As I often say to you, your best is enough. Never let anyone tell you that you must be twice as good because you are Black. Look down on no one, but look everyone in the eye as an equal. Show them sincerity. Theologian Rev. Howard Thurman once wrote, "Sincerity in human relations is equal to, and the same as, sincerity to God."[127]

Anna, Ella, and Davis, what I am asking you to do is no simple feat. Perhaps, you can draw strength from our family's history. Think of your Grandmother Ella Mae.[128] Even after being dealt a hand full of tragedy, think of how she survived with poise and grace, how she laughs. Remember, as James Baldwin wrote, you come from "sturdy, peasant stock, people who picked cotton and dammed rivers and built railroads, and in the teeth of the most terrifying odds, achieved an unassailable and monumental dignity."[129] Think of all that your bloodline has had to overcome. This is what I thought of, cradling my head in our dark basement years ago. And in the words of Baldwin, the very time I felt arrested, "my dungeon shook, and my chains fell off."

About the Author

KEVIN DEDNER serves as founder and CEO of Washington, D.C.-based Hurdle, which focuses on knocking down invisible barriers that make it harder for people of color to get the mental health care they need and deserve.

Kevin is deeply connected to Hurdle's mission, having suffered a period of depression where the biggest challenge to effective care was finding the right therapist who could truly understand and connect with his struggles as a Black man. His company's motto: **"We exist to ensure people can show up whole, operate with joy, and live with power."**

An award-winning public speaker, Kevin has over twenty years of experience in public health. A recovering politico, Kevin has worked on presidential and local political campaigns and successfully led health policy wins. He is a graduate of the University of Arkansas at Fayetteville and has a Master of Public Health from Benedictine University in Illinois. This is his debut book.

To learn more, visit: KevinDedner.com

Notes

1 Harold W. Neighbors, H. W., and James S. Jackson, "The use of informal and formal help: Four patterns of illness behavior in the black community," *American Journal of Community Psychology*, no. 6 (December 1984): 629-44. Neighbors serves as the senior scientific advisor for the National Institute on Minority Health and Health Disparities. His research and career have been devoted to studying racial, ethnic, and gender disparities in help-seeking behavior for emotional problems.

2 Ibram X Kendi, *How to Be an Antiracist* (New York: One World, 2019). Kendi discusses the biological racist ideologies that maintain, uphold, and reinforce racism. At the opening of chapter four, Kendi defines both biological racist and biological antiracist for readers. A biological racist is one who expresses the idea that the races are meaningfully different in their biology and that these differences create a hierarchy of value. Biological antiracist, contrarily, is defined as one who expresses the idea that the races are meaningfully the same in their biology and there are no genetic racial differences.

3 Janet E. Helms and Donelda Ann Cook, *Using race and culture in counseling and psychotherapy: Theory and process* (United States: Allyn & Bacon, 1999). Helms and Cook note that William Cross developed Racial Identity Functioning, a racial identity model that describes a developmental process of forming one's attitudes and beliefs about people with whom they share the same racial designation. At the lowest end of the racial identity continuum, individuals possess stereotyped attitudes about their own racial group, assume an assimilationist posture, devalue Blackness, and endorse Eurocentric notions of Blackness. In "Sacrificial Love" Kevin sees himself as superior to other Black Americans.

4 Even though Kevin's family was struggling with his father's addiction, Kevin talks about his father with an abiding sense of respect and compassion. He doesn't use disparaging language to pathologize his family situation. As Kevin's father lay dying, Kevin's mother, despite being divorced from him, worked to help him die with dignity. This loving act counters negative stereotypes of the Black family.

5 "Trauma cuts us to the core exposing the stark truth that we are fragile creatures who ultimately face death." See Stephen Joseph, What *Doesn't Kill Us: The New Psychology of Posttraumatic Growth* (Basic Books, 2011) .

6 S. A. James, "John Henryism and the health of African Americans," *Culture, Medicine and Psychiatry* 18, no. 2, (June 1994): 163-82,doi:10.1007/bf01379448. "The John Henryism hypothesis assumes that lower socioeconomic status individuals in general, and African-Americans in particular, are routinely exposed to psychosocial stressors (e.g., chronic financial strain, job insecurity, and subtle or perhaps not so subtle social insults linked to race or social class) that require them to use considerable energy each day to manage the psychological stress generated by these conditions."

7 Dahleen Glanton, "Race, the crack epidemic and the effect on today's opioid crisis," Chicago Tribune, August 21, 2017, https://www.chicagotribune.com/columns/dahleen-glanton/ct-opioid-epidemic-dahleen-glanton-met-20170815-column.html

8   "Color of coronavirus: COVID-19 deaths by race and ethnicity in the U.S.," APM Research Lab, accessed June 24, 2021, https://www.apmresearchlab.org/covid /deaths-by-race

9   Ana Sandoiu, "Racial inequities in COVID-19—the impact on black communities," *Medical News Today*, June 5, 2020, "https://www.medicalnewstoday.com /articles/racial-inequalities-in-covid-19-the-impact-on-black-communities."

10 Howard Thurman, Jesus *and the Disinherited* (New York: Abingdon-Cokesbury Press, 1949).

11 Richard G. Tedeschi, and Lawrence G. Calhoun, "Posttraumatic Growth: Conceptual Foundations and Empirical Evidence," *Psychological Inquiry* 15, no. 1, 1-18, https://doi:10.1207/s15327965pli1501_01. "Posttraumatic growth refers to the experience of positive change that occurs as a result of the struggle with highly challenging life crises." Essentially after a traumatic event, an individual might experience post-traumatic growth by gaining an increased appreciation for life, developing more meaningful interpersonal relationships, developing a sense of personal strength, experiencing a change in priorities, and/or a richer existential or spiritual life.

12 Harriette Pipes McAdoo, Black *Families* (Sage Publications, 2006). This statement addresses the notion that within many Black families, extended family members step in to help nurture children and provide support where needed. It speaks to the integrity of the Black family and extended family.

13 *Diagnostic and statistical manual of mental disorders* (American Psychiatric Association, 2013). Depressive disorders can vary in duration, symptomology and/or presumed etiology. "The common feature of all depressive disorders is the presence of sad, empty, or irritable mood, accompanied by somatic and cognitive changes that significantly affect the individual's capacity to function."

14 Joy DeGruy Leary, *Post traumatic slave syndrome: America's legacy of enduring injury and healing* (Joy DeGruy Publications, 2018). Racial socialization is the ongoing process of engaging in racial self-examination and intentional reflection on what one believes about their racial belongingness. "We have to question the images we ourselves portray. We have to examine the sounds and pictures we expose ourselves to. We have to filter what we hear on the news and strive to understand what is true."

15 John Sigal, Vincenzo F. Dinicola, and Michael Buonvino, "Grandchildren of survivors: Can negative effects of prolonged exposure to excessive stress be observed two generations later?" *The Canadian Journal of Psychiatry* 33, no. 3 (April 1988): 207-12, https://doi:10.1177/070674378803300309. Generational trauma can be defined as trauma that is "not just experienced by one person but extends from one generation to the next." One of the first studies to highlight generational trauma, also known as intergenerational trauma, was a 1988 study on the children and grandchildren of Holocaust survivors. The study found that effects of prolonged stress can have negative repercussions three generations later. The symptoms of prolonged generational trauma may include hypervigilance, anxiety, depression, and mistrust. See also: Claire Gillespie, "What is Generational Trauma? Here's How Experts Explained It," *Health*, October 27, 2020, https://www.health.com /condition/ptsd/generational-trauma.

16 "Welcome to Fulbright Elementary School," Little Rock School District, accessed
    June 24, 2021, https://www.lrsd.org/Fulbright

17 Alana Semuels, "How Segregation Has Persisted in Little Rock," *The Atlantic*,
    April 27, 2016, https://www.theatlantic.com/business/archive/2016/04
    /segregation-persists-little-rock/479538/

18 John Kirk, "Redefining the Color Line: Black Activism in Little Rock, Arkansas,
    1940 - 1970" (University Press of Florida, 2002).

19 "Racial trauma," Mental Health America accessed June 24, 2021, https://www
    .mhanational.org/racial-trauma. Studies have found that symptoms of race-based
    trauma are similar to those of individuals living with post-traumatic stress disorder.
    Nightmares are often associated with traumatic stress. Witnessing or experienc-
    ing race-based traumatic stress directly may cause individuals to have dreams or
    nightmares about the event. In other words, witnessing racial trauma can have detri-
    mental consequences on an individual's psychological health.

20 Hanif Willis-Abdurraqib, "On Paris, the Bataclan and all the young Muslims who
    still wish to dance," *Splinter News*, November 17, 2015.

21 Richard Rothstein, *The Color of Law: A Forgotten History of How Our Government
    Segregated America* (Liveright, 2017).

22 Monica N. Campbell, "Little rock, Big Impact: Centering Small Cities in U.S.
    Urban History," Hypotheses' HCA Graduate Blog, accessed June 24, 2021,
    https://hcagrads.hypotheses.org/1969.

23 Richard Rothstein, *The Color of Law: A Forgotten History of How Our Government
    Segregated America* (New York: Liveright, 2017).

24 Isabel Wilkerson, *Caste: The Origins of Our Discontents* (New York: Random House,
    2020).

25 "Little Rock, Arkansas, before 1957," C-SPAN, accessed June 24, 2021,
    https://www.c-span.org/video/?434256-3%2Frock-arkansas-1957

26 Harold W. Neighbors, and Norma L. Day-Vines, "Black Mental Health: The
    Need for Cultural Humility in Mental Healthcare, Before and After George Floyd's
    Death," *Hurdle*, accessed June 9, 2020, https://hurdle.co/wp-content
    /uploads/2021/05/Hurdle-Black-Mental-Health1.pdf;

    Matt Zoller Seitz, "The Quiet Trauma of Watching Police Brutality on Our
       Screens," *Vulture*, June 9, 2020, https://www.vulture.com/2020/06/police
       -brutality-footage-vicarious-trauma.html;

    Maria Trent, Danielle G. Dooley, and Jacqueline Dougé, "The Impact of Racism on
       Child and Adolescent Health," *Pediatrics* 144, no. 2 (August 2019),
       https://doi.org/10.1542/peds.2019-1765

27 Isabel Wilkerson, *Caste: The Origins of Our Discontents* (New York: Random House,
    2020).

    Janet Helms, Guerda Nicolas, and Carlton E. Green, "Racism and Ethnoviolence as
       Trauma: Enhancing Professional Training," *Traumatology* 16, no. 4 (December
       2010): 53-62, https://doi.org/10.1177/1534765610389595

    Thema Bryant-Davis and Carlota Ocampo, "Racist incident-based trauma," The
       Counseling Psychologist 33, no. 4 (July 2005): 479-500.

28   Joy DeGruy Leary, *Post traumatic slave syndrome: America's legacy of enduring injury and healing*, (United States: Joy DeGruy Publications, 2017). Healing generational curses and having critical conversations about race with your children is critical to their long-term mental health. Storytelling plays a critical role in Black culture and can be utilized to tell a fuller story of Black strength and the contributions Black people have made in American history. Far too often, the stories of the legacy and contributions of Black Americans are only discussed in the Black household. Nevertheless, these conversations disrupt the denial of Black greatness and provide the next generation with a true narrative about their worth.

29   Howard, Thurman, *Jesus and the Disinherited* (New York, Abingdon-Cokesbury Press, 1949).

30   Julia Ioffe, "The History of Russian Involvement in America's Race Wars," *The Atlantic*, October 21, 2017.

31   Nancy Isenberg, *White trash: The 400-year untold history of class in America* (United States: Viking, 2017).

32   Ibram X. Kendi, "Denial Is the Heartbeat of America," *The Atlantic*, January 11, 2021.

33   Angelique M. Davis, and Rose Ernst, "Racial gaslighting," *Politics, Groups and Identity* 7, no. 4 (2019): 761-74.

34   Natalie Morris, "What is 'racial gaslighting' - and why is it so damaging for people of colour?" *Metro*, June 18, 2020. Racial gaslighting is the manipulative and psychologically abusive act of denying racism and the impacts of it. As people of color experience and name racism, America continues to deny the realities. This continued denial is manipulative and psychologically abusive. Often times, individuals attempt to undermine the existence of racism by highlighting a singular practice or experience that argues the contrary. In this example, one might say, "Well-to-do white families are generous enough to donate to poor Black families, so how can racism still exist?" Racial gaslighting is also a specific type of microaggression known as microinvalidations.

35   David Margolick, "Through a Lens, Darkly," *Vanity Fair*, September 24, 2007.

36   Ta-Nehisi Coates, *Between the World and Me*, (United States, Spiegel & Grau, 2015). Amos N. Wilson, *The developmental psychology of the Black child*, (New York: Africana Research Publications, 1978).

37   James E. Marcia, "Identity and Psychosocial Development in Adulthood," *Identity* 2, no. 1 (2002): 7-28, https://doi.org/10.1207/S1532706XID0201_02. Young Black men have very limited opportunities to explore who they are. Early in life, they are told they must be aware of who they are before they even get the opportunity to discover. The media has played a problematic role in portraying one-dimensional, monolithic Black males. Kevin reflects on the role that this played in the journey to discovering himself. The opportunity to consciously and freely find oneself, as Kevin did with Uncle Glenn, is important. In that space, he essentially envisioned a new version of himself. That process alone was therapeutic. It invited him to expand his self-image. Identity development is a critical process of human development, and Black males are robbed of this humanity.

38   Howard Thurman, Howard, Jesus *and the Disinherited*, (New York: Abingdon-Cokesbury Press, 1949).

39   Arkansas Martin Luther King Jr. Commission accessed June 24, 2021, https://www
.dfa.arkansas.gov/images/uploads/budgetManuals/0318_mlking_cmsn_2007.pdf.

40   Eduardo Bonilla-Silva, Racism without Racists: Color-Blind Racism and the
Persistence of Racial Inequality in America (Maryland: Rowman & Littlefield,
2017).

41   Robin D. G. Kelly, *Freedom Dreams: The Black Radical Imagination* (Massachusetts:
Beacon Press, 2002.

42   Arkansas Times Staff, "Election 2004," *Arkansas Times*, October 22, 2004

43   American Psychiatric Association, *Diagnostic and statistical manual of mental disorders, Fifth Edition,*(Virginia: American Psychiatric Association, 2013). Dissociation
is defined as a disconnection between your thoughts, feelings, memories, actions,
and sense of identity. Dissociation can occur as the mind attempts to make sense
of competing realities. It is essentially the result of psychic trauma. One's mind
unconsciously "escapes" from the traumatic event as an attempt to cope. Repeated
stressors—such as state-sanctioned violence, community violence, death of loved
ones, and racialized trauma—can cause dissociation if other coping skills are not
exercised.

44   Debra Van Ausdale and Joe Feagin, The First R: How Children Learn Race and
Racism, (Maryland: Rowman & Littlefield, 2001).

       Isabel Wilkerson, *Caste: The Origins of Our Discontents*, (New York: Random House,
       2020).

45   Rhonda V. Magee, *The Inner Work of Racial Justice: Healing Ourselves and
Transforming our Communities Through Mindfulness,*. (United States: Tarcher
Perigee, 2019). Magee provides recommendations for healing the wounds of racial
injustice through mindfulness, introspection, and compassionate racial awareness in
an effort to achieve healthier and more meaningful connections.

46   Paul Butler, *Chokehold (Policing Black Men): A Renegade Prosecutor's Radical
Thoughts on How to Disrupt the System*, (New York: The New Press, 2017). Butler
describes at length the role of race in perpetuating state-sanctioned violence, which
is directed toward Black men. He chronicles a succession of cases and laws that perpetuate systemic racism through mass incarceration, the prison industrial complex,
police brutality (e.g., chokeholds), and the lack of prosecutorial justice for officers
that violate police policy and protocol.

47   Patrice Gaines, "Black people are in a mental health crisis. Their therapists are
busier than ever," *NBC News*, May 27, 2021, https://www.nbcnews.com/news
/nbcblk/black-people-are-mental-health-crisis-therapists-are-busier-ever-rcna1045.
Black Americans have been disproportionately impacted by the global pandemic,
especially if they earn low wages or work in service occupations as essential per-
sonnel. Individuals with substance use disorders were even more susceptible to the
virus because they had fragile organs. Many Black Americans have sought therapy
in record numbers, owing in large measure to the compounding effects of a global
pandemic and racial, economic, and political strife. Clients are experiencing fear,
lack of safety, depression, and anxiety. According to the Centers for Disease Control
and Prevention, fifteen percent of Black people seriously considered suicide.

48   Alyssa Fowers and William Wan, "Depression and anxiety spiked among black
Americans after George Floyd's death," *The Washington Post*, June 12, 2020.

49   Darrell L. Hudson, Harold W. Neighbors, Arline T. Geronimus, and James S. Jackson, "Racial discrimination, John Henryism, and depression among African Americans," *Journal of Black Psychology* 42, no. 3 (June 2016): 221-43.

50   Aimee Ortiz, "Emmett Till Memorial Has a New Sign. This Time, It's Bulletproof," *The New York Times*, October 20, 2019, https://www.nytimes.com/2019/10/20/us /emmett-till-bulletproof-sign.html

51   Isabel Wilkerson, *Caste: The Origins of Our Discontents*, (New York: Random House, 2020). The defacement of Till's memorial was a reflection of white supremacy and the eight pillars of caste, social hierarchy and terrorism.

52   "Robert E. Lee," Kappa Alpha Order, accessed June 25, 2021, https://www .kappaalphaorder.org/ka/history/lee/.

53   Jerry Mitchell, "We Found Photos of Ole Miss Students Posing with Guns in Front of a Shot-Up Emmett Till Memorial. Now They Face a Possible Civil Rights Investigation," *Propublica*, June 25, 2019, https://www.propublica.org/article /ole-miss-students-pose-with-guns-in-front-of-shot-up-emmett-till-memorial.

54   Associated Press, "Emmett Till: New memorial to Murdered teen is bulletproof," *The Guardian*, October 20, 2019, https://www.theguardian.com/us-news/2019 /oct/20/emmett-till-new-memorial-bulletproof.

55   Elizabeth Alexander, "The Trayvon Generation," *The New Yorker*, June 15, 2020, https://www.newyorker.com/magazine/2020/06/22/the-trayvon-generation.

56   Maria Trent, Danielle G. Dooley, and Jacqueline Dougé, "The Impact of Racism on Child and Adolescent Health," *Pediatrics* 144, no. 2 (August 2019), https://doi.org/10.1542/peds. Vicarious trauma involves internalizing trauma that results from witnessing acts of violence rather than being the target of it. This mental imprint can result in feelings of anger, fear, and helplessness. Moreover, exposure to race-based trauma can undermine one's sense of safety and security. The American Academy of Pediatrics defined racism as a social determinant of health that has a profound impact on the health status of ethnic minority children and adolescents. According to the AAP, chronic exposure to racialized stress increases cortisol levels, which contributes to autonomic nervous system effects, immune suppression, and heart disease, all of which put children on a trajectory to have poor physical and mental health outcomes. John Carter's death was seared into Kevin's memory.

57   "The Legend of John Henry: Talcott, WV," National Park Service, accessed June 25, 2021, https://www.nps.gov/neri/planyourvisit/the-legend-of-john-henry-talcott -wv.htm.

58   S. A. James, "John Henryism and the health of African-Americans," *Culture, Medicine and Psychiatry* 18, no. 2, (June 1994): 163-82, doi:10.1007/bf01379448.

59   Howard Thurman, *Jesus and the Disinherited* (New York: Abingdon-Cokesbury Press, 1949).

60   Steve Barnes, "Arkansas Governor Resigns After Furor," *The New York Times*, July 16, 1996, https://www.nytimes.com/1996/07/16/us/arkansas-governor-resigns -after-furor.html.

61   Michael Haddigan, "Tucker Sentenced to 4 Years' Probation," *The Washington Post*, August 20, 1996, https://www.washingtonpost.com/wp-srv/politics/special /whitewater/stories/wwtr960820.htm.

62 Paul Butler, *Chokehold (Policing Black Men): A Renegade Prosecutor's Radical Thoughts on How to Disrupt the System* (New York: The New Press, 2017).

Harold W. Neighbors,& Norma L. Day-Vines, "Black Mental Health: The Need for Cultural Humility in Mental Healthcare, Before and After George Floyd's Death," Hurdle, https://hurdle.co/wp-content/uploads/2021/05/Hurdle -Black-Mental-Health1.pdf. Kevin has persistent thoughts of countless deaths that have occurred when young people were accused of theft. This reality is reinforced in Butler's *Chokehold*, wherein he catalogues the manner in which Black Americans are hunted by the police, and in worst-cases scenarios, these interactions lead to premature death. Kevin's rumination on the dire consequences that could result in negative encounters with authority figures is a form of vicarious trauma. Kevin has not reported that he had a direct adverse encounter with the police. He does, however, describe indirect experience. He is aware that authority figures have assailed Black men and boys who ultimately lost their life as a result. This indirect exposure to violence is referred to as vicarious trauma.

63 Ella F. Washington, Alison Hall Birch, and Laura Morgan Roberts, "When and How to Respond to Microaggressions," *Harvard Business Review*, July 3, 2020, https://hbr.org/2020/07/when-and-how-to-respond-to-microaggressions.

64 "Middle School Matters: Improving the Life Course of Black Boys," *Policy Notes* 20, no. 4 (Winter 2020), https://www.ets.org/Media/Research/pdf/PICPNV20n4.pdf.

65 "Former Arkansas Governors," National Governors Association, accessed June 28, 2021, https://www.nga.org/former-governors/arkansas/.

66 Leah Cave, Matthew N. Cooper, Stephen R. Zubrick, and Carrington C. J. Shepherd, "Racial discrimination and child and adolescent health in longitudi-nal studies: A systematic review," *Social Science & Medicine* 250 (April 2020), doi:10.1016/j.socscimed.2020.112864.

67 Phillip Atiba Goff, "Consequences when African-American Boys are Seen as Older," interview by Michel Martin, *Tell Me More*, NPR, March 19, 2014, https://www .npr.org/transcripts/29140587. Dr. Phillip Atiba Goff, now professor of African-American studies and psychology at Yale, references research showing that Black boys as young as ten years old are significantly less likely to be viewed as children as their white peers. Goff explains that this contributes to the dehumanization of Black boys. Black boys are not seen as children in need of protection, punished more harshly in the criminal justice system, robbed of childhood, and forced to be conscious of the reality that they are punished as adults for their actions.

68 Phillip Atiba Goff, Matthew Christian Jackson, Brooke Allison Lewis DiLeone, Carmen Marie Culotta, and Natalie Ann DiTomasso, "The essence of innocence: Consequences of dehumanizing Black children," *Journal of Personality and Social Psychology* 106, no. 4 (April 2014): 526-45, https://doi.org/10.1037/a0035663. An emerging body of research indicates that Black boys are perceived as older,less innocent, and more likely to commit crimes, compared to their white peers. Being perceived as older increases the likelihood that children would be perceived as adults. This stereotyped behavior operates as a form of dehumanization.

69 Phillip Atiba Goff, Matthew Christian Jackson, Brooke Allison Lewis DiLeone, Carmen Marie Culotta, and Natalie Ann DiTomasso, "The essence of innocence:

Consequences of dehumanizing Black children," *Journal of Personality and Social Psychology*106, no. 4 (April 2014): 526–45, https://doi.org/10.1037/a0035663. Across four studies, Goff and colleagues found: (1) Police were less likely to perceive Black boys as children; (2) Police rated Black children and adults as less innocent than whites; and (3) Racial disparities in felonies appear to be related to the implicit dehumanization of Black people. These findings highlight the impacts of dehumanization and how it manifests to uphold systemic racism and oppression.

70   Lynette Parker, "Who let the dogs in? Antiblackness, Social Exclusion, and the Question of Who is Human," *Journal of Black Studies* 50, no. 4 (March 2019): 367-87, https://doi.org/10.1177/0021934719836421.

Harriet A. Washington, *Medical Apartheid: The dark history of medical experimentation on Black Americans from colonial times to the present* (New York: Anchor Books, 2006).

Black boys endured racist stereotypes that label them as criminals, degenerates, and uneducable, which often leads to excessive punishment. Parker addresses the notion that even dogs in U.S. society are accorded more humanity than people. Consider, for instance, that dogs are considered "man's best friend." Additionally, animal rights activists have worked to prohibit experimentation on animals. Yet in her groundbreaking book, *Medical Apartheid*, Washington catalogues the medical abuses against Black Americans from the antebellum slave period to the present. Dogs were used historically to police Black Americans (e.g., dogs used to track fugitive slaves and police dogs attacked civil rights protestors during the 1960s), which indicates the dehumanization of Black people. This inhumane exposure to violence and abusive authority causes children to lose their innocence prematurely.

71   "McDuffie Riots: Eerie Scene From Miami Race Riot Of 1980," *HuffPost*, May 29, 2013.

72   Becky Little, "How the 1982 murder of Vincent Chin ignited a push for Asian American rights," History, May 5, 2020, accessed June 28, 2021, https://www.history.com/news/vincent-chin-murder-asian-american-rights.

73   Howard Thurman, *Jesus and the Disinherited* (New York: Abingdon-Cokesbury Press, 1949).

74   Hanif Abdurraqib, *They Can't Kill Us Until They Kill Us: Essays* (Ohio: Two Dollar Radio, 2017).

75   "The Body of Emmett Till | 100 Photos" *Time*, YouTube video, 8:18, , https://www.youtube.com/watch?v=4V6ffUUEvaM.

76   "Trayvon Martin's mother, Sybrina Fulton, speaks in Portland," *The Oregonian*, YouTube video, 11:30, https://www.youtube.com/watch?v=gpzZEDyzZmU.

77   Elizabeth Scott, "How you can improve your memory when dealing with stress," Verywell Mind, February 19, 2021, https://www.verywellmind.com/stress-and-your-memory-4158323.

78   Resmaa Menakem, *My grandmother's hands: Racialized trauma and the pathway to mending our hearts and bodies* (Nevada: Central Recovery Press, 2017). Menakem addresses the impact of racism and discrimination on the mind and body. He discusses the enduring legacy of white supremacy and efforts to work through and past the trauma that engulfs Blacks and whites. Maenakem

provides recommendations for using mindfulness as one of several tools for addressing and resolving racialized trauma. Kevin's commitment to his own mental health and well-being, as well as the mental health of Black Americans broadly, is indicative of his effort to use the healing practices Menakem prescribed.

79 Neil Vigdor, "Emmett Till Sign Photo Leads Ole Miss Fraternity to Suspend Members," *The New York Times*, July 25, 2019.

80 Eliott C. McLaughlin, and Emanuella Grinberg, "Justice department reopens investigation into 63-year-old murder of Emmett Till," *CNN*, July 13, 2018, https://www.cnn.com/2018/07/12/us/emmett-till-murder-case-reopened-doj/index.html.

81 Ibram X. Kendi, *How to Be an Antiracist* (New York: One World, 2019).

82 Rebecca Joy Stanborough, "What Are Cognitive Distortions and How Can You Change These Thinking Patterns?" *Healthline*, December 18, 2019. Cognitive distortions were incorporated in psychiatrist Aaron Beck's cognitive behavioral therapy as maladaptive ways people cope with stressors. Personalization, a very common cognitive distortion that involves taking on personal blame for something that isn't your fault. Left unaddressed, racial trauma can contribute to people of color engaging in the personalization of racism. We often see this play out through gaslighting as well.

83 Bessel van der Kolk, *The body keeps the score: Brain, mind, and body in the healing of trauma* (New York: Viking, 2014). Trauma and anxiety can be accompanied by somatic symptoms such as tense muscles, chest pain, shortness of breath, headaches, and increased or irregular heart rate. Vn der Kolk underscores the impacts that trauma and anxiety have on our brain, mind and body in *The Body Keeps the Score*. The book emphasizes that traumatizing experiences impact physiological functioning. Racial trauma, whether it be vicarious or directly experienced, can have the same deleterious impacts on our mind and body.

84 Lizette Alvarez and Cara Buckley, "Zimmerman is Acquitted in Trayvon Martin Killing," *New York Times*, July 13, 2013.

85 John Couwels, and Vivian Kuo, "Zimmerman's relationship with police evolved, City files show," *CNN*, May 23, 2012, https://www.cnn.com/2012/05/23/justice/florida-teen-shooting/index.html.

86 Nicholas A. Hubbard, Joanna L. Hutchison, Monroe Turner, Janelle Montroy, Ryan P. Bowles, and Bart Rypma, ("Depressive thoughts limit working memory capacity in dysphoria," *Cognition and Emotion* 30, no. 2 (2016): 193-209, https://doi.org/10.1080/02699931.2014.991694. Kevin recalls a blurred memory and timeline during his episode of depression. Research shows that depression is linked to impaired short-term memory, such as forgetfulness and confusion. A comparative study in 2015 found that dysphoric individuals showed significantly reduced working memory compared to nondysphoric individuals.

87 "Depression in Black Americans," Mental Health America, accessed June 28, 2021, https://www.mhanational.org/depression-black-americans. Anhedonia, defined as a lack of interest and pleasure, is a symptom often associated with depression. Individuals living with depression often report losing interest in activities they've once enjoyed. Due to culture factors, however, Black American men dealing with depression might report anhedonia and irritability over feelings of sadness and

hopelessness. Social pressures, such as gender role expectations, might make Black men reluctant to report or express feelings of sadness.

88   "Excerpt from Invisible Man," University of Missouri at St. Louis, accessed June 28, 2021, http://www.umsl.edu/virtualstl/phase2/1950/events/perspectives/documents /invisibleexp.html "I am an invisible man. No, I am not a spook like those who haunted Edgar Allan Poe; nor am I one of your Hollywood-movie ectoplasms. I am a man of substance, of flesh and bone, fiber and liquids—and I might even be said to possess a mind."

89   Resmaa Menakem, *My grandmother's hands: Racialized trauma and the pathway to mending our hearts and bodies* (Nevada: Central Recovery Press, 2017). Uncle Glenn served as a role model who helped Kevin develop a sturdy constitution—one that eschewed street life. Menakem talks about the role of healthy relationships with elders, mentoring, codes of behavior as healing, and redemptive processes that work to undo trauma.

90   W. E. B. DuBois, *The Souls of Black folk* (New York: Penguin Classics, 1996). (Original work published 1903). In 1903, DuBois described competing identity structures that plague many Black Americans who were recently freed from enslavement. He wrote, "One ever feels his twoness—an American, a Negro; two souls, two thoughts, two unreconciled strivings." This quote captures the dueling identities, ambivalence, uncertainty, and inner turmoil that results from the imposition of white supremacy. White supremacy coerces many Black Americans into denying their identity and adopting an assimilationist posture that renders their authentic selves alien.

91   James E. Marcia, "Identity and Psychosocial Development in Adulthood," *Identity* 2 no. 1 (2002): 7-28, https://doi.org/10.1207/S1532706XID0201_02. Marcia's identity foreclosure is defined by high commitment to a particular identity without exploring other opportunities or options. This parallels the experience of Black people because they are not given the same chances to explore career and life opportunities in general. They are told—whether it be in an overt or covert manner—that they have to work hard, but certain spaces such as the workplace are not for them.

92   Howard Thurman, *Jesus and the Disinherited* (New York: Abingdon-Cokesbury Press, 1949). Thurman references Black resistance: "Armed resistance is apt to be a tragic last resort in the life of the disinherited. Armed resistance has an appeal because it provides a form of expression, of activity, that releases tension and frees the oppressed from a disintegrating sense of complete impotency and helplessness. 'Why can't we do something? Something must be done!' is the recurring cry."

93   "About," My Brother's Keeper Alliance accessed June 28, 2021, https://www.obama .org/mbka/about-mbka/.

94   Ibram X. Kendi, *How to Be an Antiracist* (New York: One World, 2019).

95   Faye Z. Belgrave and Joshua K. Brevard, *African American boys: Identity, culture, and development* (Springer Science + Business Media, 2015), https://doi .org/10.1007/978-1-4939-1717-4. "Racial socialization (i.e., how African American parents socialize their children about what it means to be Black in their society) affects ethnic identity development. Parental racial socialization messages contribute to higher levels of ethnic and racial identity among youth." Black boys are socialized at an early age. They are pressured to mature and follow contradicting demands to

"toughen up" for the discriminatory world they'll face yet to also remain silent and compliant. This conundrum takes place before they even get to explore the essence of who they are.

96 Faye Z. Belgrave and Joshua K. Brevard, *African American boys: Identity, culture, and development* (Springer Science + Business Media, 2015): https://doi.org/10.1007/978-1-4939-1717-4. Traditional gender roles can be problematic because they encourage men to restrict behaviors like expressing love, crying, and being vulnerable. The fact that this image of masculinity is a manifestation of white supremacy further complicates this for Black men. From origins, Black men have always been excluded from the white-developed construct of manhood and masculinity. As a result, Black men are pressured to overexert their masculinity. However, hypermasculinity has consequences on identity and development.

97 bell hooks, *We real cool: Black men and masculinity* (United Kingdom: Routledge, 2004). hooks describes the manner in which white supremacy takes an overwhelming toll on Black men. Black men are often the targets of white supremacist stereotypes and oppression. Many Black males are forced to both endure and exhibit violence, a tough persona, shame, and soul murdering. hooks calls for a cultural transformation rooted in love to counter the trauma that many Black men endure.

98 bell hooks, *We real cool: Black men and masculinity* (United Kingdom: Routledge, 2004). hooks addresses the harsh racial trauma that white supremacy imposes upon Black men. This occurs in relentless efforts to dominate and control Black men through coercive efforts such as policing, violence, soul murdering, and miseducation. The result manifests as shame, internalized oppression, substance abuse, and violence. Kevin observes both the healthy and unhealthy role models around him and works to forge his own identity—one that begins to shed the vestiges of past traumas.

99 Ibram X. Kendi, "Denial Is the Heartbeat of America," *The Atlantic*, January 11, 2021. In response to the insurrection pro-Trump rioters led at the U.S. Capitol on January 6, 2021, Kendi reflects on America's repetitive denial of its racist legacy. He cites blatant present and historical examples of racism and inequity in America—and the accompanying denial.

100 Robin D. G. Kelly, *Freedom Dreams: The Black Radical Imagination* (Massachusetts: Beacon Press, 2003).

101 Derald Wing Sue, and David Sue, *Counseling the culturally diverse: Theory and practice* (New Jersey: John Wiley and Sons Inc., 2003). Here, Kevin recalls his quest for a culturally responsive therapist. In the counseling dyad, clients should be invited to share their cultural identities and feel that their therapist provides mental health care centered around their culture and life experiences. There is a misconception that stigmas surrounding mental health in the Black community are the primary reason Black people do not engage in counseling services. Stigmas certainly play a role, but more responsibility must be directed at the lack of diversity and culturally responsive services in the mental health profession. Studies have found that fifty percent of all Black Americans terminate counseling before completing treatment, compared to thirty percent of their white counterparts.

102 Joshua N. Hook, Don Davis, Jesse Owen, and Cirleen DeBlaere, *Cultural humility: Engaging diverse identities in therapy* (Washington, D.C.: American Psychological Association, 2017). Kevin describes the cultural ruptures or impasses that occur

within therapy because counselors lack the cultural understanding to work effectively with ethnic minority clients. Hook et al. explicate a construct they refer to as "multicultural orientation," which involves: a) cultural humility or the ability to both express interest and curiosity in clients as well as the awareness that therapists may have limitations in working with clients; b) cultural opportunities or the counselor's effort to explore the client's cultural concerns; and c) cultural comfort or the counselor's ease of manner with the client.

103 Lillian Polanco-Roman, Ashley Danies, and Deidre Anglin, "Racial discrimination as race-based trauma, coping strategies and dissociative symptoms among emerging adults," *Psychological Trauma* 8, no. 5 (September 2016): 609-17.

Robert T. Carter, and Jessica Forsyth,: Reactions to racial discrimination: Emotional stress and help-seeking behaviors" *Psychological Trauma: Theory, Research, Practice, and Policy* 2, no. 3 (2010): 183-91. Persistent exposure to racism results in poor physical and mental health. Many scholars conceptualize racism as a source of race-based traumatic stress. Carter and Forsyth found that ethnic minorities who reported encounters with racism and discrimination also reported higher levels of anxiety, guilt and shame, avoidance and numbing, and hypervigilance. Kevin was able to avoid dealing with his trauma until well into his adult years. Dissociation or the disengagement from reality is a coping mechanism used to manage stress. This is a coping strategy used by many individuals who are exposed to trauma.

104 Richard J. Reddick, "We can't breathe at work, either: John Henryism and the health impact of racism," *Fortune*, June 19, 2020. "Many black professionals are hyperscrutinized on their credentials and performance, driving them to not only work harder—but also to be 'twice as good, to go half as far. . . .'"

105 "Duke University Sanford School of Public Policy Faculty" Duke University, accessed June 28, 2021, https://sanford.duke.edu/people/faculty/james-sherman.

106 Darrell Hudson., Harold W. Neighbors, Arline T. Geronimus, and James S. Jackson, "Racial discrimination, John Henryism, and depression among African Americans," *Journal of Black Psychology* 42, no. 3 (June 2016): 221-43. Studies have shown a relationship between John Henryism, or high-effort coping, and depression. It is highly possible that working hard to achieve social mobility, maintain a healthy family life, and having few support outlets may have contributed to Kevin's depression. It is also likely that unresolved trauma regarding the early loss of his father left Kevin striving for significance in ways detrimental to his mental health.

107 "Religious Landscape Study" Pew Research Center, 2019, https://www.pewforum.org/religious-landscape-study/belief-in-god/. Ninety-four percent of Black Americans are absolutely or fairly certain about their belief in God. Ninety-one percent describe religion as important or somewhat important. Only forty-seven percent of Black Americans attend church weekly. Kevin's religious foundation is challenged. He believes that God has abandoned him. Max helps him reframe his feelings of doubt.

108 Luna Greenstein, "The Mental Health Benefits of Religion and Spirituality," *National Alliance on Mental Illness*, December 21, 2016, https://www.nami.org/Blogs/NAMI-Blog/December-2016/The-Mental-Health-Benefits-of-Religion-Spiritual. Spirituality and religion play a critical role in mental health and wellness. In the Black community, spiritual and religious values have served as a refuge

and sense of hope to combat oppression. As Kevin notes, a spiritual relationship with God was one source of joy that couldn't be stolen from Black ancestors—no matter the circumstances. Spiritual and religious identities often provide individuals with hope, motivation, and determination to understand their purpose in life. Spirituality plays a critical role in the Black experience across the diaspora.

109 David H. Chae, Yijie Wang, Connor D. Martz, Natalie Slopen, Tiffany Yip, Nancy E. Adler,, Thomas E. Fuller-Rowell, Jue Lin, Karen A. Matthews, Gene H. Brody, Erica C. Spears, Eli Puterman, and Elissa S. Epel, "Racial discrimination and telomere shortening among African Americans: The Coronary Artery Risk Development in Young Adults (CARDIA) Study," *Health Psychology* 39, no. 3 (March 2020): 209–19, https://doi.org/10.1037/hea0000832. One study in 2020 found that Black Americans who reported more racial discrimination over a ten-year period showed faster signs of cellular aging. Specifically, their findings indicate that racism speeds up the shortening of telomeres. The shortening of telomeres, a repetitive sequence of DNA at the end of chromosomes to protect the cells, is associated with increased risk of heart disease, stroke, diabetes, and dementia.

110 Joseph P. Williams, "An Era of Peril for Black Mental Health," *US News*, August 13, 2020. The Centers for Disease Control and Prevention released data indicating that in June 2020, fifteen percent of Black adults had seriously considered suicide in the past thirty days, compared to about eight percent of whites. These disproportionate rates stem from a combination of crises that've impacted the mental health of Black people. In addition to the pandemic, other layered stressors—such as higher unemployment rates, higher death rates, disproportionate access to technology, limited access to health care and financial stressors—plagued Black communities.

111 Mel Kobrin, "Promoting Wellness for Better Behavioral and Physical Health," Substance Abuse and Mental Health Services Administration, accessed July 2, 2021, https://mfpcc.samhsa.gov/ENewsArticles/Article12b_2017.aspx. Substance Abuse and Mental Health Services Administration, known as SAMHSA, outlines eight dimensions of wellness: emotional, environmental, financial, intellectual, occupational, physical, social, and spiritual. Spirituality is a critical component of balanced wellness. Early on, Max reminded Kevin to lean on his faith and relationship with God for balance in his coming work with Hurdle.

112 "Research," Sidney Hankerson, accessed July 2, 2021, https://sidneyhankerson .com/research/. A growing body of research is exploring community mental health services. Community and communal work play a critical role in Black culture. Hankerson is a psychiatrist whose research focuses on providing church-based mental health services in Black communities. The practice of reimagining what it looks like to both maintain faith and access mental health care has a promising future in communities of color. Often, individuals from a background of faith report questioning their relationship with God when they experience mental illness. Mental health professionals must have the skill and competence to respond to this unique concern. Hankerson's work examines how we form and leverage the relationship between mental health professions and faith-based spaces to maximize service outcomes with this unique population.

113 Howard Thurman, *Jesus and the Disinherited* (New York: Abingdon-Cokesbury Press, 1949).

114 Stephen Joseph, *What Doesn't Kill Us: The New Psychology of Posttraumatic Growth* (New York: Basic Books, 2012). Joseph's work discusses how individuals grow as a

result of a traumatic event. Kevin allowed Joseph's work to encourage him to accept small incremental progress. He does, however, offer a critique of Joseph's work—trauma isn't a singular event for disinherited people. It's more like a collection of traumas that does not cease. This also speaks to the concerted effort it takes to maintain mental wellness as Black people. Perhaps this speaks to the strength and resilience that Black people have and must have to cope with recurring racialized stressors.

115 Harold W. Neighbors, and Norma L. Day-Vines, "Black Mental Health: The Need for Cultural Humility in Mental Healthcare, Before and After George Floyd's Death," *Hurdle*, https://hurdle.co/wp-content/uploads/2021/05/Hurdle-Black -Mental-Health1.pdf. Prevailing assumptions suggest that Black Americans eschew counseling because it is seen as the predilection of materially privileged whites. Historically, psychologists did not believe Black Americans were suitable candidates for psychotherapy because they lacked the capacity for personal insight. It is more likely, however, that therapists were either unwilling or incapable of addressing clients' specific cultural contexts.

116 Kylie M. Smith, "Discrimination and Racism in the History of Mental Health Care," National Alliance on Mental Illness, July 6, 2020, https://www.nami.org /Blogs/NAMI-Blog/July-2020/Discrimination-and-Racism-in-the-History-of -Mental-Health-Care. Medical racism has had severe impacts on mental health care. Understandably, medical mistrust has also made Black communities reluctant to access mental health services. The fields of psychiatry and psychology both have deep histories of racist practices that shape the mental health field as we know it today. In the early 1800s, for example, infamous psychiatrist Samuel Cartwright argued that Black Americans were inferior and referred to enslaved people who attempted to run away or resist labor as mentally ill. Specifically, he defined these 'tendency' as two "psychiatric" disorders—drapetomania and dysaesthesia aethiopica. Cartwright's work also influenced the scope of mental health care for Black patients. Because Cartwright argued that enslaved people were not intellectually capable of engaging in the therapeutic process, hospitals provided subpar mental health services to Black patients and assigned them duties such as custodians and kitchen staff in facilities. In the field of psychology, Black people were also viewed as inferior, excluded from research and mistreated. Furthermore, both the contributions of Black psychologists and influence of indigenous practices continue to be ignored in today's curriculum. Lastly, not until the Civil Rights Act of 1964 was it illegal to discriminate on the grounds of race in mental health care. Even after legislation was passed, many states continue discriminatory practices. In many ways, the mental health field is still learning what it looks like to exercise equitable services.

117 Barbara Brown Taylor, *Learning to Walk in the Dark* (United Kingdom: Canterbury Press Norwich, 2014). As Kevin reflects on how he has carried pain and suppressed the emotions of these pains, he starts to heal. For Kevin, therapy played a critical role in helping him "learn to walk in the dark." This process helped him come to terms with the darkness and pain that was present, is present, and will be present in the future. Nevertheless, he emerges from it with new perspective and calling. He was motivated to create a space that honors the disinherited and acknowledges their cultural needs, challenges traditional mental health practices, and ensures people show up whole, operate with joy, and live with power. Hurdle is both a symbol of Kevin's post-traumatic growth and culturally intentional mental health care for diverse populations.

118 Robert T. Carter, and Jessica Forsyth, "Reactions to racial discrimination: Emotional stress and help-seeking behaviors," *Psychological Trauma: Theory, Research, Practice, and Policy* 2, no. 3 (2010): 183-91. Carter and Forsyth found that ethnic minorities who reported encounters with racism and discrimination also reported higher levels of anxiety, guilt and shame, avoidance and numbing, and hypervigilance. Kevin's difficulty establishing emotional connections following the loss of his father at an early age likely contributed to the difficulty he experienced forging intimate relationships. Avoidant behaviors and feelings of numbness make it difficult to make emotional connections.

119 Mark Wolynn, *It Didn't Start with You: How Inherited Family Trauma Shapes Who We are and How to End the Cycle* (New York: Penguin Books, 2017). Family plays a critical role in the socialization process. Generational patterns can emerge from the experiences, pains, and traits that distant relatives portray. A grandmother's parenting style will likely influence those of mothers for generations to come. In addition, unresolved traumatic emotional wounds of parenting can be repeated through generations. "To put it simply, we receive aspects of our grandmother's mothering through our own mother. The traumas our grandmother endured, her pains and sorrows, her difficulties in her childhood or with our grandfather, the losses of those she loved who died early—these filter, to some degree, into the mothering she gave to our mother. If we look back another generation, the same would likely be true about the mothering our grandmother received."

120 Zawn Villines, "What to know about depression in Black communities" *Medical News Today*, July 27, 2020. Often times, people only associate symptoms such as anhedonia, sadness, and unproductivity with depression. Depression can be portrayed through an array of symptoms. Stigmas can also play a vital role in limiting and restricting the symptoms profile of individuals living with depression. For example, social pressures to present as masculine, restrict emotion, and "man up" influence how Black men portray feelings of hopelessness or sadness. Suppressed emotions might manifest as socially acceptable behaviors for men—such as irritability, anger, dismissiveness, and isolation.

121 Joy DeGruy Leary, Post Traumatic Slave Syndrome: America's Legacy of Enduring Injury and Healing (United States: Joy DeGruy Publications, 2018). "One of the beliefs that black people have been taught about themselves is that as a group they could not and should not trust one another. Sowing the seeds of distrust was an important tool employed by slave owners as a way of preventing slave uprisings."

122 Robert T. Carter, "Racism and Psychological and Emotional Injury: Recognizing and Assessing Race-Based Traumatic Stress," *The Counseling Psychologist* 35, no. 1, 13–105, https://doi.org/10.1177/0011000006292033. "Most mental health studies of racial discrimination and investigations of the effects of stress show that some people suffer psychological distress such as clinical depression, anxiety disorders, PTSD, or personality disorders as a result of major stressors. It is not clear, however, whether particular aspects or types of encounters with racism contribute to the psychological distress." Repeated exposure to racism and microaggressions are concerns that marginalized clients discuss in counseling.

123 Larry Buchanan, Quoctrung Bui, and Jugal K. Patel, "Black Lives Matter May Be the Largest Movement in U.S. History," *The New York Times*, July 3, 2020, https://www.nytimes.com/interactive/2020/07/03/us/

george-floyd-protests-crowd-size.html. In the summer of 2020, following the murder of George Floyd, Black Lives Matter protests peaked across nearly 550 places across the United States. Based on the data of four polls taken during the time, fifteen to twenty-six million adults protested. These reports make Black Lives Matter amongst the largest movements in U.S. history.

124 James Baldwin, *The Fire Next Time* (New York: Penguin Classics, 1990). Baldwin's quote speaks to the racial awakening and introspection that our white brothers—and sisters—must engage in to contribute to true racial healing.

125 Ibram X. Kendi, *How to Be an Antiracist* (New York: One World, 2019). Adopting an anti-racist consciousness is an active, conscious, and revolutionary process, mostly because it involves resisting the urge to deny the roles we all play in contributing to systems, beliefs, and actions that uphold racism. We must reorient ourselves to engage in the deeper understanding that leads to transformational healing. That bravery—however it might manifest—requires reorientation.

126 Carol Anderson, *White Rage* (New York: Bloomsbury, 2017). Kevin provides a socially conscious analysis about the extent to which the arbitrary construction of whiteness is used as a source of domination and control to perpetuate the myth that Black success somehow diminishes white people. Anderson provides a compelling analysis arguing that white rage directed toward Black Americans is an incendiary reaction to Black progress.

127 Howard Thurman, *Jesus and the Disinherited* (New York, Abingdon-Cokesbury Press, 1949).

128 Wade Nobles, *Seeking the Sakhu: Foundational Writings for an African Psychology* (Illinois: Third World Press, 2006). In the Black American community, the elderly hold a special position—one of elevated respect. As Nobles describes, "they represent the keepers of the family's history." Furthermore, they fulfill the role of transmitting cultural practices across generations. These practices are essential because they also illuminate the strength and resilience of the family.

129 James Baldwin, *The Fire Next Time* (New York: Penguin Classics, 1990).

CPSIA information can be obtained
at www.ICGtesting.com
Printed in the USA
BVHW060211111121
621195BV00007B/723/J